# First World War

## and Army of Occupation

# War Diary

## France, Belgium and Germany

34 DIVISION
102 Infantry Brigade
Headquarters
1 March 1918 - 28 June 1918

WO95/2461/2

The Naval & Military Press Ltd
www.nmarchive.com
**Published in association with The National Archives**

Published by

The Naval & Military Press Ltd

Unit 10 Ridgewood Industrial Park,

Uckfield, East Sussex,

TN22 5QE England

Tel: +44 (0) 1825 749494

www.naval-military-press.com

www.nmarchive.com

*This diary has been reprinted in facsimile from the original. Any imperfections are inevitably reproduced and the quality may fall short of modern type and cartographic standards.*

# Contents

| Document type | Place/Title | Date From | Date To |
|---|---|---|---|
| Heading | 34th Division. War Diary B.H.Q. 102nd Infantry Brigade March 1918 | | |
| Heading | War Diary. March. 1918. 102nd Infantry. Brigade. H.Q. | | |
| Operation(al) Order(s) | 102nd Infantry Brigade. Narrative Of Events For The Operations 21st March, 1918. | 21/03/1918 | 21/03/1918 |
| War Diary | Casualties-March 1918. | | |
| War Diary | Hamelincourt. Sheet 51B & 57C | 01/03/1918 | 02/03/1918 |
| War Diary | B.17 a 8.7. | 05/03/1918 | 07/03/1918 |
| War Diary | Hamelincourt. | 07/03/1918 | 11/03/1918 |
| War Diary | T 21b 59 | 12/03/1918 | 14/03/1918 |
| War Diary | T 2b 80 | 15/03/1918 | 19/03/1918 |
| War Diary | B4 b.26 | 20/03/1918 | 21/03/1918 |
| War Diary | B 4b.30 | 21/03/1918 | 21/03/1918 |
| War Diary | T 21d. 5.9. | 21/03/1918 | 21/03/1918 |
| War Diary | B.2d 4.9 | 22/03/1918 | 22/03/1918 |
| War Diary | S 28d.4.4. | 22/03/1918 | 23/03/1918 |
| War Diary | F 23a.8.5. | 24/03/1918 | 24/03/1918 |
| War Diary | W 2c 5.2 | 25/03/1918 | 25/03/1918 |
| War Diary | Villers L'Hopital. | 26/03/1918 | 27/03/1918 |
| War Diary | Haverskerque (Sheet 5A Hazebrouck) | 28/03/1918 | 28/03/1918 |
| War Diary | Les Lauriers. | 29/03/1918 | 30/03/1918 |
| War Diary | Estaires | 30/03/1918 | 31/03/1918 |
| War Diary | Sheet 36 | 31/03/1918 | 31/03/1918 |
| Heading | Appendices. To War Diary. Headquarters 102nd Infantry Brigade | | |
| Miscellaneous | Reference War Diary For March 1918. | | |
| Miscellaneous | Honours & Awards-March 1918. Nil. | | |
| Operation(al) Order(s) | 102nd Infantry Brigade Order No. 192 | 01/03/1918 | 01/03/1918 |
| Operation(al) Order(s) | Relief on 2/3rd March, 1918. Table A To Accompany O.O. No. 192 | 02/03/1918 | 02/03/1918 |
| Miscellaneous | Headquarters, 22nd N.F. T.S.35/318 | 06/03/1918 | 06/03/1918 |
| Miscellaneous | Headquarters, 22nd N.F. T.S.35/306 | 05/03/1918 | 05/03/1918 |
| Miscellaneous | A Form. Messages And Signals. | 05/03/1918 | 05/03/1918 |
| Operation(al) Order(s) | 102nd Infantry Brigade Order No. 193. | 05/03/1918 | 05/03/1918 |
| Operation(al) Order(s) | 102nd Infantry Brigade Order No. 194. | 06/03/1918 | 06/03/1918 |
| Miscellaneous | Relief on night March 7/8th. 1918. Table A. To accompany 102 | 07/03/1918 | 07/03/1918 |
| Operation(al) Order(s) | 102nd Infantry Brigade Order No. 195. | 11/03/1918 | 11/03/1918 |
| Operation(al) Order(s) | 102nd Infantry Brigade Order No. 196. | 18/03/1918 | 18/03/1918 |
| Operation(al) Order(s) | Table A Relief On March 19th. 1918 To accompany O.O. 193. | 19/03/1918 | 19/03/1918 |
| Miscellaneous | Ref. Map Sheet II Lens. T.S. 67/1 | 24/03/1918 | 24/03/1918 |
| Miscellaneous | Ref. Map Sheet II Lens | 25/03/1918 | 25/03/1918 |
| Miscellaneous | Table "A" To Accompany T.S 67/2 | | |
| Operation(al) Order(s) | 102nd Infantry Brigade Order No. 198. | 30/03/1918 | 30/03/1918 |
| Operation(al) Order(s) | Table "A" March on March 30th. 1918. To accompany 102nd Inf. Bde. Order 19 | 30/03/1918 | 30/03/1918 |
| Operation(al) Order(s) | 102nd Infantry Brigade Order No. 199. | 31/03/1918 | 31/03/1918 |
| Miscellaneous | Move On March 31st. Table "A" To accompany 102nd Inf. Bde. Order No. 199. | 31/03/1918 | 31/03/1918 |

| | | | |
|---|---|---|---|
| Miscellaneous | Intelligence Summary 102nd Infantry Brigade | 05/03/1918 | 05/03/1918 |
| Miscellaneous | Patrols. | | |
| Miscellaneous | Intelligence Summary 102nd Infantry Brigade. | 04/03/1918 | 04/03/1918 |
| Miscellaneous | Provisional Defence Scheme Reserve Brigade, 54th Division. | 11/03/1918 | 11/03/1918 |
| Miscellaneous | Defence Scheme-Reserve Brigade. 54th Division. Part. I | | |
| Miscellaneous | Part II. Defensive Organisation. | | |
| Miscellaneous | Appendix I. Signalling arrangements. | | |
| Heading | 34th Division. War Diary B.H.Q. 102nd Infantry Brigade April 1918. | | |
| Map | | | |
| Miscellaneous | | | |
| Heading | War Diary Headquarters, 102nd Infantry Brigade, April 1918. Vol 28 | | |
| War Diary | Erquinghem H 4.d.3.7. Sheet-36 | 01/04/1918 | 04/04/1918 |
| War Diary | B. 24 b 55.00 | 05/04/1918 | 10/04/1918 |
| War Diary | Troisrois Nieppe. | 10/04/1918 | 10/04/1918 |
| War Diary | B.29.b.55.00. | 09/04/1918 | 10/04/1918 |
| War Diary | Troisrois Nieppe. | 10/04/1918 | 10/04/1918 |
| War Diary | B.29.b.55.00 | 09/04/1918 | 10/04/1918 |
| War Diary | S 30a 5 | 12/04/1918 | 13/04/1918 |
| War Diary | S.4.a.38 | 14/04/1918 | 14/04/1918 |
| War Diary | M. 33a 6.8 | 15/04/1918 | 15/04/1918 |
| War Diary | M 29 b 59 | 16/04/1918 | 21/04/1918 |
| War Diary | 29 d 8.9 Sheet 27. | 21/04/1918 | 22/04/1918 |
| War Diary | L 1 b 9.9. | 22/04/1918 | 26/04/1918 |
| War Diary | A.20.d.4.2 | 26/04/1918 | 26/04/1918 |
| War Diary | L.I 2c.0.2. | 27/04/1918 | 30/04/1918 |
| War Diary | Casualties For The Month Of April 1918. | | |
| Heading | Honours & Awards.-April 1918. Nil | | |
| Heading | Appendices To War Diary Headquarters 102nd Infantry Brigade April 1918. | | |
| Operation(al) Order(s) | 102nd Infantry Brigade Order No. 200. | 04/04/1918 | 04/04/1918 |
| Miscellaneous | Relief on April 5/6th 1918. Table "A" To accompany 102nd Inf. Bde. Order No. 200 | 05/04/1918 | 05/04/1918 |
| Miscellaneous | 102nd Infantry Brigade Provisional Defence Scheme Left Sub-Sector 34th Divisional Front. | 03/05/1918 | 03/05/1918 |
| Operation(al) Order(s) | 102nd Infantry Brigade Order No. 201. | 20/04/1918 | 20/04/1918 |
| Operation(al) Order(s) | 102nd Infantry Brigade Order No. 202. | 21/04/1918 | 21/04/1918 |
| Miscellaneous | March Table. April 22nd 1918. To accompany O.O. No. 202 | 22/04/1918 | 22/04/1918 |
| Operation(al) Order(s) | 102nd Infantry Brigade Order No. 202. | 21/04/1918 | 21/04/1918 |
| Miscellaneous | March Table. April 22nd 1918. To accompany O.O. No. 202 | 22/04/1918 | 22/04/1918 |
| Operation(al) Order(s) | 102nd Infantry Brigade Order No. 203. | 23/04/1918 | 23/04/1918 |
| Miscellaneous | Table "A" To Accompany 102nd Inf. Bde. Order No. 203 | | |
| Operation(al) Order(s) | 102nd Infantry Brigade Order No. 204. | 27/04/1918 | 27/04/1918 |
| Miscellaneous | Intelligence Summary 102nd Infantry Brigade. | 06/04/1918 | 06/04/1918 |
| Miscellaneous | Intelligence Summary. 102nd Infantry Brigade. | 08/04/1918 | 08/04/1918 |
| Map | Croix Du Bac. | | |
| Map | Houplines. | | |
| Map | | | |
| Miscellaneous | France. | | |
| Miscellaneous | Glossary. | | |

| | | | |
|---|---|---|---|
| Heading | War Diary 102nd Infantry Brigade Headquarters, May 1918 Vol 29 | | |
| War Diary | L 12 C O.2 Sheet 27 | 02/05/1918 | 05/05/1918 |
| War Diary | K.12.d.7.8 | 05/05/1918 | 12/05/1918 |
| War Diary | B.N.a.3.2. | 12/05/1918 | 31/05/1918 |
| Miscellaneous | Casualties-May 1918. Nil. Appendix No. III | | |
| Miscellaneous | Appendix IV. 102nd Infantry Brigade. List of Honours & Rewards For May, 1918 Appendix IV | | |
| Operation(al) Order(s) | 102nd Infantry Brigade Order No. 205 | 02/05/1918 | 02/05/1918 |
| Operation(al) Order(s) | 102nd Infantry Brigade Order No. 206. App I (A) | 04/05/1918 | 04/05/1918 |
| Miscellaneous | Table "A" To accompany 102nd Inf. Bde. Order No. 206 | | |
| Operation(al) Order(s) | 102nd Infantry Brigade Order No. 207. App I (C) | 12/05/1918 | 12/05/1918 |
| Miscellaneous | Table "A" March on May 12th, 1918. | | |
| Operation(al) Order(s) | 102nd Infantry Brigade Order No. 208. App I. (a). | 12/05/1918 | 12/05/1918 |
| Miscellaneous | Table "A" Move of dismounted personnel-May 13th, 1918. | 13/05/1918 | 13/05/1918 |
| Miscellaneous | Table "B" March For transport 102nd Brigade Group-May 13th, 1918. | 13/05/1918 | 13/05/1918 |
| Operation(al) Order(s) | 102nd Infantry Brigade Order No. 209 App I (e) | 16/05/1918 | 16/05/1918 |
| Operation(al) Order(s) | 102nd Infantry Brigade Order No. 210 App. I (b) | 17/05/1918 | 17/05/1918 |
| Miscellaneous | March Table "A" To accompany 102nd Inf. Bde. Order No. 210. | | |
| Miscellaneous | Table "B" To accompany 102 Inf. Bde. Order No. 210. | | |
| Operation(al) Order(s) | 102nd Infantry Brigade Order No. 211. App I (a) | 25/05/1918 | 25/05/1918 |
| Operation(al) Order(s) | 102nd Infantry Brigade Order No. 212 App I (g) | 26/05/1918 | 26/05/1918 |
| Miscellaneous | To accompany Provisional Defence Scheme. Scheme. C. | | |
| Operation(al) Order(s) | To accompany 102 Inf. Bde. Provisional Defence Scheme. Scheme. A. | | |
| Miscellaneous | To accompany 102 Inf. Bde. Provisional Defence Scheme. Scheme. B | | |
| Miscellaneous | 102nd Infantry Brigade Provisional Defence Scheme. App II. | 06/05/1918 | 06/05/1918 |
| Miscellaneous | Cover For Documents. Nature Of Enclosures. | | |
| Heading | War Diary & Appendices June-1918 H.Qrs. 102nd Inf. Brigade. Vol 38 | | |
| War Diary | Ref. Map Sheet 3 Calais. 1/100,000. | 01/06/1918 | 05/06/1918 |
| War Diary | Ref. Map 13 Calais 1:100,000. | 06/06/1918 | 17/06/1918 |
| War Diary | Ref. Map Sheet 13 Calais 1:100,000 | 17/06/1918 | 26/06/1918 |
| War Diary | Ref. Map 13 Calais & 5a Hazebrouck 1:100,000 | 27/06/1918 | 28/06/1918 |
| Miscellaneous | Sheet 19 1:40,000. | 28/06/1918 | 29/06/1918 |
| Miscellaneous | Ref. Map. Sheet 19 & 27 1:40,000. | 29/06/1918 | 30/06/1918 |
| Miscellaneous | | | |
| Miscellaneous | Appendix No. 3 Honours & Awards-June, 1918. 22nd Bn. North'd. Fus. | | |
| Miscellaneous | 102nd Infantry Brigade Order No. 213 Appendix No.1 (a) | 02/06/1918 | 02/06/1918 |
| Miscellaneous | Distribution | | |
| Miscellaneous | 102nd Infantry Brigade Order No. 214. Appendix No. 1 (C) | 10/06/1918 | 10/06/1918 |
| Operation(al) Order(s) | Table "A" To accompany 102 Bde. Order No. 214. | | |
| Operation(al) Order(s) | 102nd Infantry Brigade Order No. 216 | 16/06/1918 | 16/06/1918 |
| Operation(al) Order(s) | 102nd Infantry Brigade Order No. 217. Appendix No. 1 (e) | 27/06/1918 | 27/06/1918 |
| Miscellaneous | 102nd Infantry Brigade Order No. 218. Appendix I (f) | 29/06/1918 | 29/06/1918 |

| | | | |
|---|---|---|---|
| Miscellaneous | March Table-To accompany 102 Inf. Bde. Order No. 218 Starting Point-Cross Roads Half Mile S. of Last E in Lederzeele. | | |
| Miscellaneous | Disposition Report. App. No. 2. | 30/06/1918 | 30/06/1918 |
| Miscellaneous | Headquarters, 34th Division. Disposition Report | 22/06/1918 | 22/06/1918 |

34th Division.

WAR DIARY

B. H. Q.

102nd INFANTRY BRIGADE.

MARCH 1918

report on Operations attached.

# WAR·DIARY·

## MARCH·1918·

## 102nd INFANTRY· BRIGADE· H·Q·

# 102nd INFANTRY BRIGADE.

## NARRATIVE OF EVENTS FOR THE OPERATIONS 21st MARCH, 1918.

MARCH 21st

4.45 a.m. Enemy opened intense bombardment of 102nd Infantry Brigade Sector with H.E. and gas. Our artillery opened S.O.S. fire and afterwards slackened to counter preparation rates.

8.15 a.m. Lieut. Nelson, 102nd Infantry Brigade, returned from 176 Infantry Brigade and reports no hostile attack on their front. Their Left Battalion was in touch with 22nd N.F. at 7.30 a.m.

8.30 a.m. Liason Officer from Brigade Headquarters arrives at H.Q. 23rd N.F. slightly wounded. 23rd N.F. report still no sign of enemy attack.

8.50 a.m. 23rd N.F. report not in touch with battalion on left since 8.10 a.m.

9 a.m. About 9 a.m. enemy reported to have attacked Division on our right and driven them back.

9.55 a.m. Report from 59th Division that enemy was advancing. Our artillery ordered to fire S.O.S. again.

10 a.m. Between 9.30 a.m. and 10 a.m. right company 22nd N.F. was driven our of their front line trench. A defensive flank was formed along GOLLIWOG LANE - VALLEY SUPPORT - PELICAN AVENUE. Enemy reported in our front trench between GOLLIWOG LANE and BORDERER LANE but 22nd N.F. held Southern portion of BORDERER LANE.

11.30 a.m. 1 Company 25th N.F. placed at disposal of O.C. 22nd N.F. for the protection of his right flank in case of emergency. About this time the enemy made several bombing attacks along our front trench on the right but was driven off with loss each time.

11.45 a.m. Pigeon message, timed 11 a.m. from LUCAS O.P. addressed QRT (R.F.A. Bde. 59th Div.) was brought in. Message stated that enemy was on ridge N.W. of BULLECOURT.

12 noon. Officers patrol 1st East Lancs. sent to ascertain situation on ridge N.W. of ECOUST. Liason Officer (Lieut. Nelson, 102nd Inf. Bde.) previously sent to H.Q. 176 Infantry Brigade returned at 12 noon with a report that enemy was believed to be in RAILWAY RESERVE in C.4.b. and C.5.a. about 11 a.m. 176th Infantry Brigade believed to be holding TOWER RESERVE - TANK RESERVE and FOX TROT LANE. 35 casualties in Reserve Company 22nd N.F. from artillery and machine gun fire up to 12 noon.

12.40 p.m. Pigeon message timed 11.55 a.m. from LUCAS O.P. addressed QRT was brought in. Message stated enemy was advancing in large numbers from BULLECOURT towards ECOUST.

1 p.m. 22nd N.F. in touch with all Companies.

/ About 1 p.m. ..

About 1 p.m. 1 Company 1st Bn. E. Lancs. Regt. was ordered to form a defensive flank facing S.E. through U.25.c. and B.6.b. As the enemy was advancing in U.25.a., the 2 left companies 25th N.F. moved to about T.21.Central ready to counter attack Southwards and 1 other company took up a position along the bank in U.25. S.E. where they had 25% casualties from hostile attack.

1.20 p.m. 34th Division report ECOUST held by enemy. O.C. 1st E. Lancs ordered to go and see G.O.C. 176th Infantry Bde. at L ' HOMME MORT with a view to co-operating in a counter attack on ECOUST to be carried out by 176th Infantry Brigade. This counter attack did not materialise.

1.30 p.m. Headquarters, 22nd N.F. moved to North of LEG LANE.

1.45 p.m. Troops 102nd Infantry Brigade compelled by pressure of enemy attacks to withdraw from GOLLIWOG LANE to MARS LANE.

2 p.m. Troops 23rd N.F. reported still holding out in TUNNELL TRENCH.

2.30 p.m. Enemy attacks along our front line trench drove our men from MARS LANE into VALLEY SUPPORT near QUEEN'S LANE.

3.15 p.m. Enemy advanced in rear of VALLEY SUPPORT. Troops 22nd N.F. fell back up QUEEN'S LANE and occupied TIGER TRENCH near QUEEN'S LANE at 3.45 p.m.

3.30 p.m. Right Company 23rd N.F. withdrew its front line platoons to BURG SUPPORT and established a block in BURG SUPPORT about 30 yards East of QUEEN'S LANE. This company then engaged the enemy who were advancing from the South with rifle and Lewis gun fire. At 3.30 p.m. R.E. operators of Listening Apparatus at U.19.b.5.4. left (after destroying apparatus) having received no messages since 11 a.m.

4 p.m. 22nd and 23rd N.F. were gradually forced back along TIGER TRENCH and STRAY RESERVE to FACTORY AVENUE: a position about the junction of TIGER TRENCH and KNUCKLE AVENUE was held for a short time.

In FACTORY AVENUE details of 22nd and 23rd N.F. prolonged the line already held by troops 101st Infantry Brigade Westwards to the junction with NELLY AVENUE.

During the afternoon the enemy penetrated into T.30. and T.29.b and d advancing in the direction of CROISILLES. An observer (Lieut. Finlayson, Lovat scouts) in a tree near Brigade Headquarters reported ~~ve.ry~~ very large numbers of the enemy (several thousand) in the low ground in T.30. during the afternoon.

J Special Coy. R.E. came under the orders of G.O.C. 102nd Infantry Brigade and held the front line, Third system just South of ST. LEGER wood in the afternoon.

Troops 103rd Infantry Brigade, in addition to 1st E. Lancs, arrived during the afternoon and occupied the front line Third system across the SENSEE VALLEY and also South of ST. LEGER wood

4.20 p.m. 102nd Infantry Brigade Pioneer Company was ordered to occupy CROISILLES SWITCH in T.29.b and d and to join up with troops 25th N.F. about T.23.d.

O.C. 25th N.F. reported by telephone from BUNHILL ROW at 4.20 p.m. that the enemy were in the sunken road parallel with BUNHILL ROW in U.25.b. and asked for them to be shelled. Soon after this telephonic communication with Battalion Headquarters in BUNHILL ROW broke down and could not be restored on account of the presence of the enemy in MAIDA VALE.

5 p.m. About 5 p.m. Lieut. Colonel, S. Acklom, D.S.O., M.C attempted to fight his way out towards CROISILLES but was killed. His Acting Adgt., Lieut. Moyes, succeeded in getting through.

5.30 p.m. M.O. 23rd N.F. still at Aid Post in U.19.b. and cleared all wounded before leaving at this time. He reports that the men in the trenches East of the Aid Post (i.e. about QUEEN'S LANE and KNUCKLE AVENUE) withdrew towards CROISILLES.

8.30 p.m. Troops 102nd Infantry Brigade in FACTORY AVENUE withdraw (together with troops 101st Infantry Brigade in that trench) to the front line second system between T.18.c.6.4. and T.17.d.6.9. The enemy attacked T.18.c.6.4. but was driven off

About 9 pm. Orders issued for 102nd Infantry Brigade to hold front line Third system and CROISILLES SWITCH NORTH as follows :-

T.22.b.6.0. - sunken road T.23.a.6.6. (exclusive) 102 Bde. Pioneer Coy.

Sunken road T.23.a.6.6. inclusive to sunken road T.17.c.8.2. inclusive J Special Coy. R.E.

T.17.c.8.2. - junction of CROISILLES SWITCH NORTH - and front line second system at T.17.d.6.9. - including details of all units 102nd Infantry Brigade under Capt. Mc.Lachlan, 25th N.F.

About 10.30 pm. Brigade Headquarters moved to T.21.d.5.9.

March 22nd -

3.20 a.m. Orders issued for portion of CROISELLES SWITCH NORTH from its junction with 3rd system at T.22.d.3.9. to T.23.a.5.0. to be taken over by 1st East Lancs.

103rd Infantry Brigade orders 10th Lincolns to take over this portion of the line as 1st East Lancs. could not arrive before dawn.

Major Neeve, 23rd N.F. placed in Command of Composite Battalion comprising all details 102nd Infantry Brigade includ-:ing 102nd Brigade Pioneer Coy. and "J" Special Coy. R.E.

6.0 a.m. Brigade Headquarters moved to B.2.d.4.9.

9.25 am. Hostile M.G's very active; enemy reported forming up in CROISELLES. Asked Division to have CROISILLES shelled.

Hostile shelling heavy on S. slopes of HENIN HILL.

10.25 am. Reported that no hostile attack had devloped on our front. It appeared later that enemy had attacked and broken through about the road T.23.a.4.6. but that the details 102nd Infantry Brigade under Capt. Mc.Lachlan had counter attacked and re-established the line.

11.30 am. Report received that enemy had attacked from CROISELLES and forced troops on HENIN HILL back into Support Line of Second System.

"B" Company 18th N.F. in billets in SENSEE VALLEY, B.3.a. was ordered to occupy and hold HILL SWITCH.

This Company was placed under orders of Major Neeve.

12.30 pm. HILL SWITCH was held from T.22.b.5.0. (in touch with 103rd Infantry Brigade) Northwards with Left in touch with 101st Infantry Brigade.

At 1.0 p.m. some of the troops on the left of 102nd Inf. Bde. front retired and a defensive flank was formed by "B" Coy. 18th N.F. from T.16.b.3.5. to T.21.b.7.7. facing N.W. The enemy held HILL SWITCH North of T.16.b.3.5.

About 3·0 p.m. - During the afternoon the enemy delivered heavy attacks on ST. LEGER, and about 5.0 p.m. was reported to have entered that village.

5·10 p.m. - The details under Major NEEVES withdrew to front line 3rd System in T.21·c. Touch was kept with 10th Lincolns on right but there were no British troops on immediate left.

6.0 p.m. - Brigade H.Q. opened at MOYENNEVILLE.

7.0 p.m. - Advanced Brigade H.Q. opened at T.22.a.2.8.

8·10 p.m. - Orders issued for relief of details 102nd Inf. Brigade and attached troops by parts of 4th Guards Brigade and 93rd Infantry Brigade.

March 23rd -

Relieving troops commenced to arrive about dawn March 23rd.

10.0 a.m. - G.O.C. 102nd Infantry Brigade handed over Command of the front held by 102nd Inf. Bde. details and attached troops to 93rd Inf. Bde. through O.C. 13th West Yorks.

Relief complete at about noon except for about 200 men in T.8. who were relieved at 10·0 p.m.

---

[illegible signature]
Major
Bde Major 102 Inf Bde.

## C A S U A L T I E S - MARCH 1918.

| U N I T. | K I L L E D. Offr. | O.R. | W O U N D E D. Offr. | O.R. | M I S S I N G. Offr. | O.R. | T O T A L. Offr. | O.R. |
|---|---|---|---|---|---|---|---|---|
| 22nd Bn. North'd. Fus. | 2 | 31 | 5 | 61 | 10 | 455 | 17. | 547. |
| 23rd Bn. North'd. Fus. | - | - | 1 | 57 | 17 | 364 | 18. | 421. |
| 25th Bn. North'd. Fus. | 1 | 21 | 6 | 131 | 10 | 281 | 17 | 433. |
| 102nd L.T.M.B. | - | - | 1 | 4 | 1 | 11 | 2 | 15. |
| | 3 | 52 | 13 | 253 | 38 | 1111 | 54 | 1416 |

Army Form C. 2118.

# WAR DIARY
*or*
# INTELLIGENCE SUMMARY.
*(Erase heading not required.)*

Instructions regarding War Diaries and Intelligence Summaries are contained in F. S. Regs., Part II. and the Staff Manual respectively. Title pages will be prepared in manuscript.

Volume 28

HQ 102 Inf Bde.

March 1918

| Place | Date | Hour | Summary of Events and Information | Remarks and references to Appendices |
|---|---|---|---|---|
| HAMELINCOURT Sheets 51B & 57C | 1st | | O.O. 192 issued | Appendix 1(a) |
| " | 2nd | | 102 Inf Bde relieved 178th Inf Bde in the line (Right Section Centre Sector) in accordance with OO 192. | |
| B.17a8.7 | 5th | | O.O. 193 issued | Appendix 1(b) |
| " | | | Reliefs carried out & Brigade front extended in accordance with OO 193 | |
| " | 6th | | O.O. 194 issued | Appendix 1(c) |
| " | 7th | | 102nd Inf Bde was relieved in the line by 103 Inf Bde and moved into Div Reserve in accordance with OO 194. Relief complete 1-30am Mar 8th | |
| HAMELINCOURT | | | | |
| " | 10th | | Part III Provisional Defence scheme for Reserve Brigade 34 Div issued | Appendix 2 |
| | | | Precautionary period 'CAREFUL' (vide Defence Scheme) ordered from 10pm. | |
| " | 11th | | Parts I, II and Appendix 1 to Defence Scheme issued | Appendix 2 |
| | | | O.O. 195 issued | Appendix 1(d) |
| T21d5.9 | 12th | | Moves carried out in accordance with OO 195. | |
| " | 14th | 10.50pm | 'BATTLE' (vide Defence Scheme) ordered. | |
| T26b8.0 | 15th | 10am | Bde HQ moved to T26b8.0. | |

2353 Wt. W2544/1454 700,000 5/15 D. D. & L. A.D.S.S./Forms/C. 2118.

Army Form C. 2118.

# WAR DIARY
*or*
~~INTELLIGENCE~~ SUMMARY.

*(Erase heading not required.)*

Instructions regarding War Diaries and Intelligence Summaries are contained in F. S. Regs., Part II. and the Staff Manual respectively. Title pages will be prepared in manuscript.

HQ 102 Inf Bde — March 1918

| Place | Date | Hour | Summary of Events and Information | Remarks and references to Appendices |
|---|---|---|---|---|
| T26 8.0. | 19th | | 102nd Inf. Bde. relieved 103rd Inf Bde in Right Subsector in accordance with OO196. Complete 9-50pm | |
| B4b.26. | 20th | | On night 20/21st counter preparation B was fired by all guns and hows. on possible enemy forming up places | |
| " | 21st | 5 am | The enemy opened an intense bombardment of H.E. and gas shell on our front system at 5 am. St LEGER was also shelled at this time. Bde HQ moved to HQ Right Group RFA | |
| B4b.30 | " | 5.5 am | B 4b.3.0. at 5.5 am | |
| | " | 9 am | about 9am the enemy attacked. narrative of events ~~attached~~ [illegible] | [illegible] |
| T21d.5.9. | " | | about 10pm BdeHQ moved to T21 d.5.9 | |
| B.2d.4.9. | 22nd | 5 am | Bde HQ moved to B2d.4.9. | |
| S28d.4.4 | " | 5pm | Bde HQ moved to MOYENNEVILLE S28.d.44. | |
| | | | Adv. Bde HQ established at T27a 2-8. about 7pm. | |
| | | | Relief of 34th Div by 31st Div commenced. Troops 102 Inf Bde assembled at MOYENNEVILLE | |
| " | 23rd | | Co. 18th NF and J special Co. RE rejoined their units. Relief of 102nd Inf Bde complete at 3pm except for 5 off. and 200 men in front line third system south of BOIRY BECQUERELLE who were relieved about 10pm. | |
| " | | 4pm | 102nd Inf Bde marched to camp just North of ABLAINZEVILLE F23a.8.5 sheet 57D. | |

2353 Wt. W2544/1454 700,000 5/15 D. D. & L. A.D.S.S./Forms/C. 2118.

Army Form C. 2118.

# WAR DIARY
*or*
~~INTELLIGENCE SUMMARY~~.
*(Erase heading not required.)*

Instructions regarding War Diaries and Intelligence Summaries are contained in F. S. Regs., Part II. and the Staff Manual respectively. Title pages will be prepared in manuscript.

HQ 102 Inf Bde — March 1918

| Place | Date | Hour | Summary of Events and Information | Remarks and references to Appendices |
|---|---|---|---|---|
| F23 a.8.5. | 24th | | 102nd Inf. Bde marched to BAILLEULMONT ~~at~~ leaving ABLAINZEVILLE at 3.30 pm. Disposition on arrival. Bde HQ W2c5.2 (Sheet 51c). 22 NF, 25 NF, 102 LTMB BAILLEULMONT 23 NF BERLES AU BOIS | |
| W2c5.2 | 25th | | 102nd Inf Bde marched to LIGNEREUIL area leaving BAILLEULMONT at 9.15 am. Disposition on arrival. Bde HQ and 102 LTMB. the Chateau LIGNEREUIL. 22 NF BEAUFORT. 23 NF LIGNEREUIL. 25 NF DENIER. | |
| VILLERS L'HOPITAL | 26th | | 102nd Inf Bde marched to VILLERS L'HOPITAL leaving LIGNEREUIL at 9.30 am. all units billetted in VILLERS L'HOPITAL. Bde HQ was established in house next to the Church. Piquets were established on the FROHEN LE GRAND - DOULLENS road at the Eastern edge of FROHEN LE GRAND, ~~and~~ on the VILLERS L'HOPITAL - BONNIERES and VILLERS L'HOPITAL - FROHEN LE GRAND road just outside VILLERS L'HOPITAL. | |
| | 27th | | 102nd Inf Bde (less a proportion of transport) marched to FREVENT station and entrained there in the early morning of March 28th. Proportion of transport marched to VALHOUN | |
| HAVERSKERQUE (Sheet 5A HAZEBROUCK) | 28th | | 102nd Inf Bde detrained at STEENBECQUE station and marched to billets. Bde HQ, 23 NF, 25 NF 102 LTMB in HAVERSKERQUE, 22 NF in TANNAY. Proportion of transport marched to CHOCQUES | |
| LES LAURIERS | 29th | | 102nd Inf Bde marched to billets as follows:- Bde HQ LES LAURIERS K14d9.1 (Sheet 36A) 22 NF ARREWAGE; 23 NF LA RUE DU BOIS E22; 25 NF CAUDESCURE: 102 LTMB K14c. | |

Instructions regarding War Diaries and Intelligence Summaries are contained in F. S. Regs., Part II. and the Staff Manual respectively. Title pages will be prepared in manuscript.

Army Form C. 2118.

# WAR DIARY
*or*
~~INTELLIGENCE SUMMARY.~~
*(Erase heading not required.)*

HQ 102 Inf Bde — March 1918.

| Place | Date | Hour | Summary of Events and Information | Remarks and references to Appendices |
|---|---|---|---|---|
| LES LAURIERS | 30th | | 102nd Inf Bde marched to ESTAIRES area. Disposition on arrival. Bde HQ L29b.4.3. | |
| | | | 22 NF, 25 NF, 102 LTMB ESTAIRES; 23rd NF NEUF BERQUIN. | |
| ESTAIRES | | | While in ESTAIRES area 102nd Inf Bde was in Corps Reserve XV Corps. | |
| " | 31st | | 102nd Bde marched to ERQUINGHEM area and came into Divisional Reserve 34 Div. | |
| Sheet 36. | | | Disposition on arrival. | |
| | | | Bde HQ. H4d.3.7. | |
| | | | 22 NF H4d95.45 | |
| | | | 23 NF H11c.6.4 | |
| | | | 25 NF H5a45.70. | |
| | | | 102 LTMB. ERQUINGHEM. | |

E. W. Thomson Brig Genl
Comdg 102 Inf Bde

2353 Wt. W2544/1454 700,000 5/15 D. D. & L. A.D.S.S./Forms/C. 2118.

# Appendices to War Diary

# Headquarters
## 102nd INFANTRY BRIGADE

Reference War Diary for March 1918.

Some of the Operation Orders that were issued are not attached, having been lost or destroyed in the operations near ST. LEGER.

for B. [illegible] Major

BRIGADIER GENERAL.
COMMDG. 102nd INFANTRY BRIGADE.

**HONOURS & AWARDS - MARCH 1918.**

N I L.

SECRET. Copy No.. 16

**102nd INFANTRY BRIGADE ORDER No.. 192**

Ref. Maps
Sheets
51.B.S.W. Edn. 7.C.
(Provisional) &
51.C. N.W.

1 : 3 : 1918.

1. The 102nd Infantry Brigade will relieve 178th Infantry Brigade in the Right Section, Centre Sector, VI Corps front on the night 2/3rd March, 1918, in accordance with the attached Table A.

2. Machine Guns in Right Section are being relieved on night 3/4th March by 103rd M.G. Coy. and 4 guns 102 M.G. Coy. under Divisional arrangements. 4/3 March

3. Battalions will move from their present Camps to H.Q. of Battalions in the line by Companies at 10 minutes interval; forward of the H.Q. of battalions in the line by parties not greater than platoons at not less than 100$^{x}$ distance.
A distance of 100$^{x}$ will be maintained between battalions and their transport.

4. All defence schemes, aeroplane photographs, trench maps, reserve S.A.A., grenades, L.T.M.B. bombs, Very lights, S.O.S. grenades, anti-gas appliances and all other trench and area stores will be taken over by units on relief.
Lists of stores taken over will be forwarded by each unit to Brigade Headquarters by 3.0 p.m. March 3rd.

5. All information about the enemy and details of work in hand and proposed will be taken over by each unit on relief.

6. All other details of relief will be arranged direct between C.O's concerned.

7. Units on taking over will be disposed exactly as is 178th Infantry Brigade at present, and the general policy of defence will not be departed from. Any minor alterations which it may be desired to make after completion of the relief will be reported to Brigade Headquarters.

8. Completion of relief will be reported to Brigade Headquarters B.17.a.8.7. by telegraphing the code word "LION".

9. 102nd Infantry Brigade Headquarters will close at HAMELINCOURT at 6.0 p.m. March 2nd and reopen at L'HOMME MORT, B.17.a.8.7. at the same hour.

10. G.O.C. 102nd Infantry Brigade will assume Command of the Right Section on completion of the relief on night 2/3rd March.

Acknowledge.

[signature]
Major
BRIGADE MAJOR
102nd INFANTRY BRIGADE.

Issued at 7 pm. to -

| | |
|---|---|
| G.O.C. ............ Copy No. 1 | 208th Field Co. R.E. .. Copy No. 11 |
| Brigade Major ..... " " 2 | Brigade Supply Officer. " " 12 |
| Staff Captain. .... " " 3 | 103rd Field Ambulance.. " " 13 |
| Bde. Signals ...... " " 4 | Diary and File ....... Copies Nos. 14 & 15 |
| Bde. Transport Officer .... 5 | H.Q. 34th Division ... " " 16 |
| T.O. 20th N.F. .... " " 6 | H.Q. 101st Inf. Bde .. " " 17 |
| 22nd N.F. ......... " " 7 | H.Q. 103rd Inf. Bde. .. " " 18 |
| 23rd " ......... " " 8 | |
| 25th " ......... " " 9 | |
| 102 L. T. M. B. ... " " 10 | |

-----

Relief on night 2/3rd March, 1918. Table A To accompany O. O. No.. 191

| Serial No. | UNIT | Relieves | In | Guides | | ROUTE | REMARKS. |
|---|---|---|---|---|---|---|---|
| | | | | Place | Time | | |
| 1 | 102 L.T.M.B. | 178 L.T.M.B. | Right Section. | - | - | ST. LEGER - CROISILLES. | Relief to be completed before dusk. |
| 2 | 23rd N.F. | 7th SHERWOOD FORESTERS. | Right Sub-section. | L'HOMMEMORT B.17.a.8.7. | 6.0 pm | No restriction. | |
| 3 | 25th N.F. | 2/5th SHERWOOD FORESTERS. | Left Sub-Section. | - do - | 6.45 pm | " | |
| 4 | 23rd N.F. | 2/6th SHERWOOD FORESTERS. | Brigade Reserve. | - do - | 7.15 pm | " | |

**SECRET.**

T.S.35/318

Headquarters,
22nd N.F.
23rd N.F.
25th N.F.
102 L.T.M.B.

-----

34th Division : for information.
103rd Infantry Bde.:

------

Cancel T.S.35/306 dated the 5th inst. and substitute the following -

Reference 102 Infantry Brigade Order No.193, from the completion of the relief on night 5/6th March, the inter-battalion boundary in Right Section 34th Division front will be as follows -

U.15.d.5.5. -VULCAN MEBU (inclusive to Right Sub-Section), JOVE LANE -QUEENS LANE - LEG LANE all inclusive to Left Subsection, thence T.30.a.0.5.- corner of wood T29c70

B. [signature]
Major,
BRIGADE MAJOR,
102nd INFANTRY BRIGADE.

6: 3: 1918.

S E C R E T

Headquarters,
22nd N.F.
23rd N.F.
25th N.F.
102 L.T.M.B.
--
34th Division.
103rd Infantry Bde.
--

T.S.35/306

Reference 102 Infantry Bde. Order No. 193, from the completion of the relief on night 5th/6th March, the inter-battalion boundary in Right Section, 34th Division front will be as follows -

U.15.d.5.5. - VULCAN MEBU (inclusive to Right Sub-section), JOVE LANE - QUEENS LANE - LEG LANE all inclusive to Left Subsection, thence U.25.a.0.0. - T.30.d.0.0.

Major.
BRIGADE MAJOR.
102nd INFANTRY BRIGADE.

5-3-1918

"A" Form.

Army Form C.2121 (in pads of 100).

No. of Message

## MESSAGES AND SIGNALS.

Prefix ... Code ... m. | Words | Charge | This message is on a/c of: ... Service, (Signature of "Franking Officer.") | Recd. at ... m. Date ... From ... By ...

Office of Origin and Service Instructions. Secret

Sent At ... m. To ... By ...

TO 34 Div

| Sender's Number. | Day of Month. | In reply to Number. | AAA |
|---|---|---|---|
| * BM 797 | 5 | | |

Ref attached order please note that the Co. H.Q. and one of the support platoons which are at present in the front line just North of HUMP Lane will be accommodated in BURG SUPPORT on this Brigade taking over the new front tonight

B. L[illegible] Major

for Brig. General

Cmdg 102 Inf Bde



From 102 Bde

Place

Time

The above may be forwarded as now corrected. (Z) Censor. Signature of Addressor or person authorised to telegraph in his name.

* This line should be erased if not required.

750,000. W 2138 ... H. W. & V., Ld. 6/16.

SECRET.

Copy No..

## 102nd INFANTRY BRIGADE ORDER No. 193

14

Ref. Maps
FONTAINE and
CROISILLES
Sheets, 1:10,000.

5 : 3 : 1918.

1.. The front of the Right Section 34th Div. front will be extended Northwards to-night 5/6th March.

2.. From the completion of the relief detailed below the Northern boundary of the Right Section will be the line from a point midway between posts 4 and 5 in the front line (U.14.a.33.85), junction of JUNO LANE and TUNNEL Trench thence along JUNO LANE and FACTORY AVENUE both inclusive to Right Section to GUARDIAN RESERVE, thence to first line of second system where it crosses the CROISILLES--FONTAINE CROISILLES road T.18.c.65.45 (road exclusive to Right Section) - thence along CROISILLES--ST LEGER Road to T.29.a.0.5. (road and river at this point exclusive to Right Section.)

3.. The Left Brigade has the right to use FACTORY AVENUE as well as the Right Brigade.
NELLY AVENUE is entirely for the use of the Left Brigade.

4. 25th Bn. N.F. will take over the extension of this Brigade front from 15th ROYAL SCOTS to-night.
The Company 25th Bn. N.F. now in Battalion Reserve in first line of second system will be used for this purpose.
Relief not to commence before 6.15 p.m.

5. On completion of the relief this Company 25th Bn. N.F. will be disposed as follows :-

| | |
|---|---|
| Coy. H.Q. ..... | BURG SUPPORT. |
| 2 platoons .... | Front line posts 1, 2, 3 and 4. |
| 2 platoons .... | in support in BURG SUPPORT between HUMP LANE and JUNO LANE. |

6.. All reserve S.A.A., grenades, S.O.S. signal lights, rations, water, and all other trench stores, will be taken over on relief. Lists of stores taken over will be forwarded by 25th Bn. N.F. to Brigade Headquarters by 3.0 p.m. March 6th.
Aeroplane photographs, information about the enemy and details of work in hand and proposed will also be taken over on relief.

7.. All other details of the relief will be arranged direct between C.O's concerned.

8.. Completion of the relief will be reported to Brigade Head-:quarters by telegraphing the word "TIGER".

9.. G.O.C. 102nd Infantry Brigade will assume Command of the extension of the front of the Right Section on completion of the relief to-night.

10.. From 3.0 p.m. March 5th. the Battalion in Brigade Reserve will earmark one of its Companies accommodated in and West of the railway embankment T.24.d., to hold the first line of the second system from the road junction T.24.b.5.2. to the Northern boundary of the Right Section (T.18.c.65.45.) in case of hostile attack.
This Company will not be moved from this position in case of hostile attack without orders from Brigade Headquarters.

Acknowledge.

Issued at 3 pm to -



K. Lidwitz
Major.
BRIGADE MAJOR.
102nd INFANTRY BRIGADE.

| | | | |
|---|---|---|---|
| G.O.C. ..... | Copy No. 1 | 25th Bn. N.F. ......... | Copy No. 8 |
| Brigade Major | " " 2 | 102nd L.T.M.B. ....... | " " 9 |
| Staff Captain | " " 3 | 208th Fld. Co. R.E. | " " 10 |
| Signals | " " 4 | 18th Bn. N.F. (for A Coy.) | " " 11 |
| Bde. Transport Off. | " 5 | Diary and File ... | Copies 12 & 13 |
| 22nd N.F. | 6 | H.Q. 34th Div. | 14 |
| 23rd " | 7 | 101st Inf. Bde. | 15 |

SECRET.

Copy No.. 10

102nd INFANTRY BRIGADE ORDER No .. 194.

6 : 3 : 1918

Ref. Maps
CROISILLES &
FONTAINE Sheets
1:10,000 -
Sheet 57.C. 1:40,000.

1. The 102nd Infantry Brigade will be relieved in the line by 103rd Infantry Brigade on the night 7/8th March, 1918, in accordance with attached Table A.

2. On relief 102nd Infantry Brigade will move to the HAMELINCOURT--ERVILLERS Area and will be in Divisional reserve.

3. Guides from units 102nd Infantry Brigade at the rate of 1 per Company and 1 per Battalion Headquarters will meet relieving units at Brigade Headquarters B.17.a.8.7. In the case of battalions taking over the front line 1 guide per platoon and 1 per Company Headquarters will be provided by units at their Headquarters.

4. All moves East of RAILWAY RESERVE will be by platoons at 100x interval. West of RAILWAY RESERVE minimum distances of 100x between Companies and 100x between battalions and their transport will be maintained.

5. All defence schemes, aeroplane photographs, trench maps, reserve S.A.A., grenades, L.T.M. bombs, S.O.S. signals, and all other trench stores will be handed over on relief. Receipted lists of stores handed over will be forwarded to Brigade Headquarters by 12 noon March 9th.

6. All information about the enemy and details of work in hand and proposed will be handed over on relief.

7. Units 102nd Infantry Brigade will each send advance parties not exceeding one Officer and 5 O.R's per battalion to take over billets in the Reserve Brigade Area at 3.0 p.m. March 7th.

8. All other details of relief will be arranged direct between O.C's concerned.

9. Completion of relief will be reported to Brigade Headquarters by telegraphing the word 'LEOPARD'.

10. Command of the Right Section will pass to G.O.C. 103rd Infantry Brigade on completion of the relief.

11. Brigade Headquarters will close at B.17.a.8.7. on completion of relief and reopen at HAMELINCOURT, A.5.b.3.2. at the same hour.

Acknowledge.

H. Lobridge
Major.
BRIGADE MAJOR.
102nd INFANTRY BRIGADE.



Issued at p.m.

| | | | | |
|---|---|---|---|---|
| G.O.C. ...... | Copy No. 1 | 101st Inf. Bde. .. | Copy No. | 11 |
| Brigade Major | " " 2 | 103rd Inf. Bde. .. | " " | 12 |
| Staff Captain | " " 3 | H.Q. 177th Inf. Bde. .. | " " | 13 |
| Signals .... | " " 4 | Right Group R.F.A. .... | " " | 14 |
| Bde. T.O. ... | " " 5 | 208th Fld. Co. R.E. .... | " " | 15 |
| 22nd N.F. .. | " " 6 | 'C' Co. 34th Div. M.G. Bn. | " " | 16 |
| 23rd " .. | " " 7 | No. 3 Coy. Div. Train .. | " " | 17 |
| 25th " .. | " " 8 | Brigade Supply Officer .. | " " | 18 |
| 102 L.T.M.B.. | " " 9 | 104th Field Ambulance ... | " " | 19 |
| H.Q. 34th Division | " 10 | | | |

Diary and File ...... Copies 20 and 21

***

Relief on night March 7/8th. 1918. TABLE A. To accompany 102 Inf. Bde. Order No. 194.

| Serial No. | UNIT | Relieved By | In | Time for guides at D.17.a.8.7. | DESTINATION | ROUTE | Takes over Camp from | REMARKS |
|---|---|---|---|---|---|---|---|---|
| 1 | 102 L.T.M.B. | 103 L.T.M.B. | Right Section. | - | INNISKILLING CAMP, ERVILLERS. | CROISILLES: ST. LEGER. | - | Relief to be complete by dusk. O.C. 25th N.F. will allot accommodation in INNISKILLING CAMP. |
| 2 | 23rd N.F. | 10th LINCOLNS. | Brigade Reserve. | 6.0 p.m. | CLONMELL CAMP HAMELINCOURT. | By decauville train. | 10th LINCOLNS | 103rd Inf. Bde. Q.M. Stores will also be in CLONMELL CAMP. |
| 3 | 22nd N.F. | 1st EAST LANCS. | Right Subsection. | 6.45 p.m. | BELFAST CAMP ERVILLERS. | No restriction. | 1st EAST LANCS. | |
| 4 | 25th N.F. | 9th (N.H.) N.F. | Left Subsection. | 7.30 p.m. | INNISKILLING CAMP, ERVILLERS. | ditto | 9th (N.H.) N.F. | |

SECRET

Copy No.. 10

# 102nd INFANTRY BRIGADE ORDER No ... 195.

11 : 3 : 1918.

1. From information received it appears probable that the enemy may launch an attack on VI Corps front on the morning of March 13th.

2. The moves laid down in Reserve Brigade Provisional Defence Scheme, 34th Division Part III, under "BATTLE PERIOD" with the exception of para. 10 will be carried out commencing at 6.0 p.m. March 12th unless the code word "BATTLE" should be circulated prior to that hour.
Orders for the move of transport will be issued later.

3. Completion of all moves mentioned in para. 2 above will be reported to Brigade Headquarters, T.21.d.5.9. by telegraphing the code word 'PUMA'.

4. This order in no way modifies the state of readiness ordered in T.S. 35/335 dated 10th March.

5. Brigade Headquarters will close at HAMELINCOURT at 6.0 p.m. and reopen at T.21.d.5.9. at the same hour.

Acknowledge.

Major
BRIGADE MAJOR.
102nd INFANTRY BRIGADE.

Issued at 7/30pm to :-

| | |
|---|---|
| G.O.C. ........... | Copy No. 1 |
| Brigade Major .... | ' ' 2 |
| Staff Captain .... | ' ' 3 |
| Signals ......... | ' ' 4 |
| Bde. Transport Off. | ' ' 5 |
| 22nd N.F. ........ | ' ' 6 |
| 23rd " ........ | ' ' 7 |
| 25th " ........ | ' ' 8 |
| 102 L.T.M.B. ..... | ' ' 9 |
| 34th Division .... | ' ' 10 |
| 101st Inf. Bde ... | ' ' 11 |
| 103rd Inf. Bde ... | ' ' 12 |
| 208th Fld. Co. R.E. | ' ' 13 |
| 181st Tunnelling Co. R.E. | ' 14 |

Diary and File .... Copies 15 & 16.

Secret.

Copy No.. 10

# 102nd INFANTRY BRIGADE ORDER No.. 196

Ref. Maps
Sheets
57.C. N.W. &
51.B. S.W. - 1:20,000

18 : 3 : 1918.

1. The 102nd Inf. Bde. will relieve 103rd Inf. Bde. in the Right Subsector, 34th Div. front, on March 19th in accordance with the attached Table A.

2. All moves will be by parties not greater than platoons at not less than 200 yds. interval. Should hostile balloons be up or enemy aeroplanes about, troops will move off the roads as far as possible.
   No transport will be sent forward until dusk except Lewis Gun limbers which may go as far as ST. LEGER only by day.

3. Units 103rd Inf. Bde. are providing guides at the rate of 1 per platoon for battalions taking over the line and 1 per Company for the reserve battalion.

4. All defence schemes, aeroplane photographs, reserve S.A.A., grenades and all other trench stores will be taken over by units on relief: also all information about the enemy and details of work in hand and proposed.
   Units 102nd Inf. Bde. will hand over to units 103rd Inf. Bde. on relief, the Reserve Brigade Defence Scheme, T.S. 35/342 dated March 11th (Memorandum on Counter attacks), details of the reconnaisances carried out with a view to possible action in case of hostile attack (including relief of permanent garrisons of Front line, Second System, in BUNHILL ROW and HENIN HILL, and the occupation of CROISILLES SWITCHES NORTH and SOUTH): also all trench shelters, area stores and the extra S.A.A., grenades, flares, etc. issued to the men to complete their equipment to the scale laid down in Provisional Defence Scheme, Reserve Brigade, Part III, para. 6.
   Lists of stores handed over and taken over will be forwarded by each unit to Brigade Headquarters by 6.0 p.m. March 20th.

5. Units 103rd Inf. Bde. are sending advance parties to take over bivouacs, etc. on the morning of March 19th.



/ 6.. All other ..

6. All other details of relief will be arranged direct between C.O's concerned.

7. Completion of relief will be reported to Brigade Headquarters by telegraphing the word 'B E A R'.

8. 102nd Inf. Bde. Headquarters will close at T.2.b.8.6. at 8.30 p.m. March 19th and reopen at B.4.b.2.6. at the same hour.

9. G.O.C. 102nd Inf. Bde. will assume Command of the Right Subsector on completion of the relief.

Acknowledge. Sd

B. Lethbridge
Major.
BRIGADE MAJOR.
102nd INFANTRY BRIGADE.

Issued at 2 pm to :-

| | |
|---|---|
| G.O.C. ............. | Copy No. 1 |
| Brigade Major ...... | " " 2 |
| Staff Captain ...... | " " 3 |
| Signals ............ | " " 4 |
| Bde. Transport Off... | " " 5 |
| 22nd N.F. ......... | " " 6 |
| 23rd " ......... | " " 7 |
| 25th " ......... | " " 8 |
| 102 L. T. M. B. ..... | " " 9 |
| 34th Division ...... | " " 10 |
| 101st Inf. Bde ...... | " " 11 |
| 103rd Inf. Bde ...... | " " 12 |
| Right Group R.F.A. .. | " " 13 |
| 'C' Co. 34th Bn. M.G.C. .......... | " " 14 |

Diary and File .. Copies 15 & 16.

TABLE A – RELIEF ON MARCH 19th. 1918. To accompany O.O. 193.

| Serial No. | UNIT | RELIEVES | IN | GUIDES | | ROUTE | Hand over bivouacs to | REMARKS. |
|---|---|---|---|---|---|---|---|---|
| | | | | Place | Time leading platoons to arrive. | | | |
| - 1 | 102 L.T.M.B. | 103 L.T.M.B. | Right Subsector. | To be arranged by O.C's batteries. | | ST. LEGER– CROISILLES. | 103 L.T.M.B. | Relief to be complete before dusk. |
| 2 | 23rd N.F. | 10th LINCOLNS. | Left Section | Bn. H.Q. U.25.a.7.5 | 5.0 p.m. | T.20.a.0.5.– JUDAS FARM– ST. LEGER– CROISILLES. | 10th LINCOLNS | Company to be in Battalion Reserve to load. |
| 3 | 25th N.F. | 9th N.F. | Brigade Reserve. | Bridge over road T.20.a. 40.75. | 6.0 p.m. | JUDAS FARM – ST. LEGER – CROISILLES. | 9th N.F. | |
| 4 | 22nd N.F. | 1st. E. LANCS. | Right Section. | Bn. H.Q. U.25.b.8.2 | 7.0 p.m. | ST. LEGER – CROISILLES. | 1st. E. LANCS. | |

SECRET

T.S. 67/1

Ref. Map
Sheet 11 LENS.

24 : 3 : 18.

1. 34th Division is marching to LE CAUROY Area tomorrow, March 25th.

2. 102nd Brigade Group will march as follows :-

| Troops in order of march. | Starting Point. | Time of passing. | Destination. |
|---|---|---|---|
| Bde. H.Q. & 102 L.T.M.B. | Road Junction ¼ mile N.E. of BAILLEULMONT CHURCH. | 10.30 a.m. | LIGNEREUIL |
| 25th N.F. | - ditto - | 10.32 a.m. | DENIER |
| 22nd N.F. | - ditto - | 10.36 a.m. | BEAUFORT |
| 23rd N.F. | - ditto - | 10.40 a.m. | LIGNEREUIL |

3. ROUTE -

GOUY - FOSSEUX - BARLY - AVESNES LE COMTE - APPEGRENEE - LIGNEREUIL.

4. All transport will march brigaded in rear of the column under the Brigade Transport Officer.

5. Distances of 200 yards will be maintained between the battalions and between the transport of battalions on the march.

6. Billetting parties 23rd N.F., 25th N.F. and 102 L.T.M.B. (mounted on horses or bicycles) will meet the Staff Captain at BAILLEULMONT CHURCH at 10.0 a.m.

Billetting parties 22nd N.F. will be at the CHURCH, LIGNEREUIL, at 12 noon and await the arrival of the Staff Captain there.

7. Arrival in billets and position of Headquarters will be reported by units to Brigade Headquarters.

8. Units will be prepared to entrain on 26th instant.

9. 102nd Field Ambulance is marching independently to BEAUFORT tomorrow, 25th instant.

10. Acknowledge by bearer.

Major.
BRIGADE MAJOR.
102nd INFANTRY BRIGADE.

24 : 3 : 1918.

Addressed - 22nd N.F.
23rd "
25th "
102 L.T.M.B.
Signals.
Staff Captain.

34 Div. for information

SECRET

Ref Map
Sheet 11 LENS.

B.M.37/2

25 : 3 : 1918

1. 102nd Brigade Group will march to the VILLERS L'HOPITAL area tomorrow, March 26th in accordance with the attached Table A.

2. Transport will march with units.

3. 400 yards distance will be maintained between battalions on the march.

4. In addition to the usual 10 minutes halts there will be a long halt of about 1½ hours about mid day.

5. Billeting parties of units 102nd Infantry Brigade will proceed independently to meet the Staff Captain at the Church VILLERS L'HOPITAL at 1 p.m. 102nd Field Ambulance will make their own arrangements for billets with the Town Major, AUXI LE CHATEAU.

6. Arrival in billets and position of H.Q. will be reported by each unit of the Group to Brigade Headquarters.

7. 102nd Field Ambulance is arranging to collect sick from units by 8.30 a.m.

ACKNOWLEDGE BY BEARER.

(signature)
Major.
BRIGADE MAJOR.
102nd INFANTRY BRIGADE.

Addressed - 22nd N.F.
23rd N.F.
25th N.F.
102 L.T.M.B.
Staff Captain.
Signals.
102nd Field Ambulance.

34th Division .. for information.

Table "A" To accompany [illegible]

| Troops in order of march. | Starting place | Time to pass. | Route | Destination. |
|---|---|---|---|---|
| [illegible] N.F. | Road junction at S end of DENIER village. | 9.45 a.m. | [illegible] [illegible] FREVENT BONNIERES | VILLERS L'HOPITAL |
| Bde. H.Q. 10[illegible] L.T.M.B. | Cross roads at last L in LIGNEREUIL | 9.50 am | DENIER thence as for [illegible] N.F. | VILLERS L'HOPITAL |
| 23rd N.F. | Cross roads at last L in LIGNEREUIL | 9.5[illegible] a.m. | As for Bde. H.Q. | VILLERS L'HOPITAL |
| * 22nd N.F. | Cross roads at [illegible] | 9.2[illegible] a.m. | LIENCOURT [illegible] thence as for Bde. H.Q. | VILLERS L'HOPITAL |
| 102nd Field Amb. | Cross roads at [illegible] | 9.37 a.m. | As for 22nd N.F. | AUXI LE CHATEAU |

* Joins column at [illegible]

SECRET. Copy No..

10

# 102nd INFANTRY BRIGADE ORDER No.. 198.

Ref. Map
Sheet 36.A.
1:40,000.

30 : 3 : 1918.

1. The 102nd Infantry Brigade will march to-day March 30th to the ESTAIRES Area in accordance withe the attached Table 'A'.

2. While in the ESTAIRES Area, 102nd Infantry Brigade will be in Divisional Reserve to 57th Division in Right Sector XVth Corps front.

3. Advance parties to take over billets will report to the Town Major, ESTAIRES, or the Sub-Area Commandant, NEUF BERQUIN, at 12 noon March 30th acording to the Village in which they are to be billeted.

4. Distances of 200 yds. between Companies and between the rear of units and their transport will be maintained on the march.

5. Arrival in billets and position of Headquarters will be reported by each unit to Brigade Headquarters.

6. Brigade Headquarters will close at Les LAURIERS at 2.0 p.m. Reports during the march to the head of the column on the MERVILLE--ESTAIRES Road.

Acknowledge.

[signature]
Major
BRIGADE MAJOR.
102nd INFANTRY BRIGADE.

Issued at 7.30 a.m. to :-

| | | |
|---|---|---|
| G.O.C. .. | Copy No. | 1 |
| Brigade Major | " " | 2 |
| Staff Captain | " " | 3 |
| Signals | " " | 4 |
| Bde. Transport Off. | " | 5 |
| 22nd N.F. | " | 6 |
| 23rd " | " | 7 |
| 25th " | " | 8 |
| 102 L.T.M.B. | " | 9 |
| 34th Division | " | 10 |
| 57th Division | " | 11 |
| Town Major, ESTAIRES | " | 12 |
| Sub-Area Comdt. NEUF BERQUIN ......... | " | 13 |

---

File and WarDiary ... 14 & 15.

TABLE "A". March on March 30th. 1918.

To accompany 102nd Inf. Bde. Order.. 1[illegible]

| Serial No. | UNIT | Starting Point: Place | Starting Point: Time to pass | ROUTE | DESTINATION | REMARKS |
|---|---|---|---|---|---|---|
| 1 | Bde. H.Q. & 102 LTMB. | Cross Roads K.15.c.4.2. | 2.0 p.m. | MERVILLE—CHAPELLE DUVELLE. | ESTAIRES | |
| 2 | 22nd N.F. | Road Junction K.16.b.1.9. | 2.5 p.m. | - do - | ESTAIRES. | |
| 3 | 25th N.F. | Road Junction K.4.c.2.4. | 2.10 pm. | - do - | ESTAIRES. | |
| 4 | 23rd N.F. | Road Junction E.17.d.9.0. | 2.0 pm. | LA COURONNE. | NEUF BERQUIN. | |

S E C R E T. Copy No.. 14

# 102nd INFANTRY BRIGADE ORDER No... 199.

Ref. Maps.
Sheets 36 & 36.A.
1:40,000.

31 : 3 : 1918.

1. 34th Division is relieving 38th Division in the Left Sector XVth Corps front. (Front line from I.20.d.5.2. to River LYS ar C.16.b.7.5.)
 101st Infantry Brigade took over the Left (HOUPLINES) Subsector on night 30/31st March, and 103rd Infantry Brigade is to take over the Right (WEZ MACQUART) Subsector on the night 31st March/1st April.

2. 102nd Infantry Brigade will march to-day 31st March to the ERQUINGHEM Area in accordance with the attached Table A and take over billets to be vacated by units 103rd Infantry Brigade.

3. While in the ERQUINGHEM Area, 102nd Infantry Brigade will be in Divisional Reserve (to 34th Division).

4. Advance parties to take over billets, etc. will be sent by each unit 102nd Infantry Brigade to arrive at the H.Q. of the unit 103rd Infantry Brigade concerned at 3.0 p.m. to-day.

5. All moves will be by Companies at 200 yds. distance.

6. Units 102nd Infantry Brigade will take over from units 103rd Infantry Brigade ~~the Reserve Brigade Defence Scheme (Left Division XVIth Corps front) and~~ all Area and billet stores.
 Lists of stores taken over will be forwarded to Brigade Head:quarters by 3.0 p.m. April 1st.

7. Completion of all moves will be reported to Brigade Head:quarters.

8. Brigade Headquarters will close at ESTAIRES at 5.0 p.m. and reopen at ERQUINGHEM H.4.d.3.7. at the same hour.

Acknowledge.

Major
BRIGADE MAJOR
102nd INFANTRY BRIGADE.

Issued at 7.30 a.m. to :-

| | | |
|---|---|---|
| G.O.C. ..... | Copy No. | 1 |
| Brigade Major | " " | 2 |
| Staff Captain | " " | 3 |
| Signals | " " | 4 |
| Bde. Transport Off.. | " " | 5 |
| 22nd N.F. | " " | 6 |
| 23rd " | " " | 7 |
| 25th " | " " | 8 |
| 102nd L.T.M.B. | " " | 9 |
| 34th Division .. | " " | 10 |
| 57th Division .. | " " | 11 |
| 101st Inf. Bde. | " " | 12 |
| 103rd Inf. Bde. | " " | 13 |

Diary and File ... Copies 14 & 15.

MOVE ON MARCH 31st. TABLE "A". To accompany 102nd Inf. Bde. Order No. 199.

| Serial No. | UNIT | Starting Point | | ROUTE | DESTINATION | Takes over billets from | REMARKS. |
|---|---|---|---|---|---|---|---|
| | | Place | Time to pass | | | | |
| 1. | Bde. H.Q. | Bridge over R. LYS at G.25.d.9.6. | 6.15 p.m. | BAC ST MAUR. | ERQUINGHEM. | - | |
| 2. | 102 L.T.M.B. | ditto. | 6.20 p.m. | ditto. | ERQUINGHEM. | 103rd L.T.M.B. | |
| 3. | 22nd N.F. | ditto. | 6.30 p.m. | ditto. | ERQUINGHEM. | 1st E. LANCS. H.Q. H.4.d.95.45. | |
| 4. | 25th N.F. | ditto. | 7.0 p.m. | ditto. | ERQUINGHEM LAUNDRIES. | 10th LINCOLNS H.Q. H.5.a.45.70. | |
| 5. | 23rd N.F. | ERQUINGHEM CHURCH. | 7.15 p.m. | ditto. | LA ROLANDERIE. | 9th (N.H.) N.F. H.Q. H.11.c.6.4. | |

CONFIDENTIAL

## INTELLIGENCE SUMMARY
## 102nd INFANTRY BRIGADE
### From 9 a.m. 5-3-1918 to 9 a.m. 6-3-1918

A. OUR OPERATIONS

1. Artillery -
Our artillery was more active than usual. Bursts were fired at frequent intervals by 18 pdrs. and 4.5 Hows. on HENDECOURT, CRUMP ALLEY (U.15.c.), TRIDENT ALLEY (U.15.d.) and COPSE TRENCH.

2. Trench Mortars - Nil.

3. Machine guns -
Harassing fire was directed on the following targets - Tracks in U.16.Central and U.15.b., Sunken road in U.16.c.

4. Aircraft -
Our 'planes were fairly active during the day. Flights were made over hostile lines but in all cases they met with hostile A.A. and M.G. fire.

B. ENEMY ACTIVITY

1. Artillery -
Hostile artillery also displayed greater activity during the period. BORDERER LANE, STAFFORD LANE, and VALLEY SUPPORT were shelled at frequent intervals (77 mm.)

| | | | |
|---|---|---|---|
| 10 am - 11 am | .... 18 rds. (4.2) | ... | U.21.c. |
| 1 pm - 2 pm | .... 8 rds. (5.9) | ... | Near No. 7 Post (U.21.a.50.15). |
| 9 p.m. | .... 6 rds. (4.2) | ... | PELICAN LANE. |

2. Trench Mortars - Nil.

3. Machine guns -
Hostile machine guns were slightly active on the right subsector, but inactive on the left. A hostile M.G. is reported about U.21.a.90.90. (No sign of a M.G. emplacement at this point is visible on recent aeroplane photographs).

4. Aircraft -
Enemy formations were active over his own lines.

C. INTELLIGENCE

1. Movement -

7.10 am .. 14 men each carried a piece of timber (12' by 4' by 2' approx) from dump at U.10.d.95.40. They disappeared into TRIDENT ALLEY at U.16.c.30.70.

7.15 to 7.30 am .. 3 parties of 12 men stood on parapet of HOP LANE (U.6.d. and V.1.c.)

7 am to 9 am .. Much movement around Northern end of CROWS NEST

8.30 am .. 2 men standing in CRUX TRENCH (U.16.c.)

11 am .. 2 parties of 12 men per party carried timber from dump at U.10.d.95.48. and entered CRUX TR. (U.16.a.

3.45 pm .. 14 men, in full marching order proceeded along road (U.11.d.20.80.) and entered HENDECOURT.

4 pm .. 3 men carrying boxes (1' sq. approx) left CROWS NEST and entered HENDECOURT.

4.30 to 5 pm .. 20 men carrying tins similar to petrol tins left SPANIEL ALLEY (U.16.c. b & d) and proceeded to HENDECOURT. Partly returned shortly still carrying the tins.

2. Work -

8.15 am .. Small enemy working party in U.18.b. dispersed by Lewis gun fire.

3. Transport -

3. Transport -
7 am .. 5 wagons moving N.E. on DURY - HENDECOURT ROAD.
8 am .. 7 " " " " " " "
9.40 am . 1 wagon drawn by 6 horses proceeded N.E.on DURY - HENDECOURT road. This wagon came from the direction of CROWS NEST.
5.25 pm. .6 wagons moved S.W. along DURY - HENDECOURT road through U.6.c. and d.

4. Miscellaneous.-
Right Battn. reports - Sounds as of heavy tractors in the direction of HENDECOURT. This occurred at 7.40 p.m. and 4.5 am Unloading of heavy material was also heard.

Left Battn. reports - Noises were heard from the direction of HENDECOURT. The noise was similar to that of a drilling machine.

From snipers report _ Muffled sounds as of hammering was heard between 7 and 8 am. It appeared to come from enemy's front line about U.15.a.

[signature]
Major.
BRIGADE MAJOR
102nd INFANTRY BRIGADE.

9-5-1918

# P A T R O L S.

about 11pm

1.. An Officers patrol reconnoitred VULCAN ALLEY and CRUMP ALLEY (U.15.c) Nothing was seen or heard of the enemy. The wire around U.15.c.90.50. was examined and found to be in good condition.

2.. A patrol of 1 Officer and 14 O.Rs. with a Lewis Gun left No.5 Post (U.21.a.93.21) at 10.15.p.m. About 150 yards beyond our own wire 2 of the enemy were seen. On seeing our patrol they ran immediately. The T head at U.21.b.Central was then reconnoitred and found to be unoccupied. No signs of recent occupation were visible and the trench was under water in places. 50 yards S.E of T head an unoccupied listening post was discovered. A track ran between this trench and the post.

Sounds similar to a pertrol engine were distinctly heard in the enemy's line ab ut this time. The patrol saw no further signs of the enemy.

3.. The sunken road from U.15.c.05.15. to U.14.d.98.35. was patrolled by 1 Officerand 1 Sniper between 10.30.am and 12.15.p.m but no signs of the enemy were seen. The road is a mass of shell holes and hard to locate. The nearest enemy wire in this part is at least 200x East of the road. The head of a German sentry and smoke of his rifle were seen in COPSE TRENCH about U.15.a.15.95. On being fired at by our snipers he disappeared and was not seen again.

4.. A patrol of 1 Officer and 2.O.R. reconnoitred the BULLECOURT Road near FAG ALLEY just before 7.a.m. The road is much ~~destroyed~~ damaged.

CONFIDENTIAL

## INTELLIGENCE SUMMARY
## 102nd INFANTRY BRIGADE.
From 9 a.m. 4-3-1918 to 9 a.m. 5-3-18

---

A. OUR OPERATIONS

1. Artillery -
Our 18 pdrs. carried out a shoot on the junction of COPSE TR. and TRIDENT ALLEY (U.18.c.0.4.). COPSE TRENCH, CRUX TRENCH and HENDECOURT were intermittently shelled.

2. Trench Mortars -
3. Machine guns -
4. Aircraft -
.. Nil.

B. ENEMY OPERATIONS

1. Artillery -
Hostile artillery was quiet throughout the period. Our support line was occasionally shelled. Twenty shells fell in the vicinity of QUEENS LANE, all of which were 'duds'.

1a. Gas -
During the evening three gas shells fell near the Left Battn. H.Q. (U.25.a.7.5. No effects of gas were felt.

2. Trench Mortars - NIL.

3. Machine guns -
Hostile machine guns were inactive; occasional bursts were fired at morning 'stand to'. A hostile gun appeared to be firing from the junction of DOG TRENCH and TRIDENT ALLEY.

4. Aircraft - Nil.

C. INTELLIGENCE

1. Movement -

8.[illegible] am ... 2 men standing for 5 minutes at U.18.b.90.40. Trench at U.18.b.80.50. was then entered.

11 am ... 3 men standing on parapet of CRUX TRENCH looking towards our line.

11.45 am ... 6 men left COPSE TRENCH and disappeared at U.18.b.80.30.

2. Signals -
At 5.30 a.m. a signalling lamp was active from about U.18.d.4.4.

---

- PATROLS -

1. A patrol leaving No. 10 POST proceeded along FAG ALLEY until reaching the sunken road at U.14.b.45.50. Here it remained for a considerable time but nothing was seen or heard of the enemy.

2. At 5.0 a.m. a patrol left our lines and reached a point U.14.c.9.2. The patrol then moved 20X in a Southerly direction and listened for any enemy movement.
No sounds were heard nor movement seen.

/ 3.. An Officers

3.. An Officers patrol reached point U.15.c.30.30. Nothing was seen or heard of the enemy.

4.. A fighting patrol of 1 Officer and 28 other ranks left No. 5 POST (U.21.a.35.25.) at 9.30 p.m. On arriving at U.21.b.35.80 the patrol halted. Talking and sounds as if work was in progress could be heard from the direction of DOG TRENCH. Very lights were fired from the ' T' Head trench at U.21.b.45.55. No hostile patrols were encountered.

5.. A patrol of 1 Officer and 9 O.R's left our lines at 1.30 a.m. and proceeded along the sunken road in U.15.c. At U.15.c.55.20 patrol listened and sounds were heard in a N.W. direction about 30$^{x}$ distant. A bell also was heard ringing. The patrol advanced to this spot and a party of the enemy were seen moving rapidly away. Fire was opened on them but no identifications were secured.

[signature] for Major
BRIGADE MAJOR
102nd INFANTRY BRIGADE.

5:3:1918.

SECRET

## PROVISIONAL DEFENCE SCHEME

## RESERVE BRIGADE, 34th DIVISION.

Distribution -

| | |
|---|---|
| G.O.C. .................... | Copy No. 1 |
| Bde. Major ................ | " 2 |
| Staff Captain ............. | " 3 |
| 102 Bde. Signals .......... | " 4 |
| Bde. Transport Officer .... | " 5 |
| 22nd N.F. ................. | " 6 |
| 23rd N.F. ................. | " 7 |
| 25th N.F. ................. | " 8 |
| 102 L.T.M.B. .............. | " 9 |
| 34th Division ............. | " 10 |
| 101st Infantry Bde. ....... | " 11 |
| 103rd Infantry Bde. ....... | " 12 |
| 208th Field Coy. R.E. ..... | " 13 |
| 181st Tunnelling Coy. R.E.. | Part III only. |

Map "A" has been issuod to Units 102nd Infantry Brigade only.

---

T.S.35/338

Horowith Parts I and II and Appendix I, Copy No. ....
Provisional Dofonco Schomo, Reserve Brigade, 34th Division.

Ploaso acknowledgo rocoipt.

B. [signature]

Major.
BRIGADE MAJOR.
102nd INFANTRY BRIGADE.

11-3-1918

SECRET.

Copy No..

# DEFENCE SCHEME - RESERVE BRIGADE.

## 34th DIVISION.

: PART I :

1. Extent of Divisional Front -

The 34th Division holds the Centre Sector VI Corps front. The 59th Division on the Right and the 3rd Division on the left hold the line on the flanks of 34th Division.

The 34th Division front extends from N.W. of BULLECOURT ( U.21.central) to the FONTAINE LES CROISILLES--HENINEL road in U.1.b.central.

2. Organisation of Divisional Area -

The Divisional front is organised in two Subsectors, each held by 1 Infantry Brigade.
1 Infantry Brigade is in Divisional Reserve in the HAMELINCOURT--
--ERVILLERS Area.

3. Boundaries - (see Map A)

Southern Divisional Boundary -
U.19.c.7 . - Front line at U.21.b.2.0. - PELICAN AVENUE (inclusive to Centre Sector) - U.26. .25.48 - I.30.d.0.0. to HALLY COPSE (inclusive to Centre Sector).

Northern Divisional Boundary -
U.1.b.50.45 - Front line at U.1.a.3.3. - T.3.a.45.65 - T.5.central - T.1.a.0.0. (Brigade H.Q. at T.2.b.8.0. inclusive to Centre Sector).

Boundary between Brigades in the line -
U.14.a.45.80 - junction of JUNO and TUNNEL trenches - thence along JUNO (inclusive to Right Brigade) to its junction with BURG SUPPORT - thence along FACTORY AV. to GUARDIAN RESERVE - thence to 1st line of 2nd system at the point where it crosses the CROISILLES -- FONTAINE LES CROISILLES road (T.18.c.35.45) road inclusive to Left Brigade, thence along CROISILLES--ST.LEGER road to the road junction T.23.d.15.75. - thence to road junction T. .c.central.
Both Brigades in the line have the right to use FACTORY AV.: NELLY AV. is entirely for the use of the Left Brigade.

4. Important Tactical features in the Divisional Area -

(a) Front system -
The spur North of BULLECOURT on which are two rises known as the "KNUCKLE" U.20.a. and the "HUMP" U.14.c. The loss of this spur would give the enemy observation to the West especially up the CROISILLES--ST.LEGER railway and railway from ECOUST to CROISILLES.

The open basin North of CROISILLES (T.12.). It is of importance that the enemy should not be able to force an entrance into this basin on a front broad enough to enable him to turn the defences on the CHERISY spur in U.1.a. and c. and T.3.

(b) Second system -
The tactical localities which it is essential to hold are -
(i)... The spur North West of ECOUST.
(ii)... The spur immediately South of CROISILLES.
(iii)... The spur immediately North of CROISILLES.
[illegible]

## : PART II :

### Defensive Organisation -

1. The defences on the Army front are organised into -

    (a) The Forward Zone.
    (b) The Battle Zone.
    (c) The Rear Zone.

The limits of these zones are shown on Map A.

2. The Forward Zone consists of Front, Support and Reserve Lines comprising the First system.

3. The Battle Zone consists of the Second and Third Systems with switches between them.
Each of these systems will eventually consist of Front, Support and Reserve lines.

4. The rear Zone will eventually consist of at least one complete system of trenches connected by switches to the Third system.

### Responsibility for Defence -

5. The Division is responsible for the defence of the Forward Zone and of the forward edge of the Battle Zone (front trench of First system).

### Functions of the Zones of defence -

6. The functions of the Forward Zone (First system) are to guard against surprise, to break up the enemy's attack and to compel him to expend large quantities of ammunition and employ large forces for its capture.

7. The Battle Zone has been selected with a view to our main resistance being made on ground favourable to us.

### General Principles of Defence -

8. Forward Zone -
The line of main resistance is the Reserve line i.e. TIGER TRENCH--STAFFORD LANE--HUMP SUPPORT--LINCOLN RESERVE--SENSEE RESERVE.
Should the enemy penetrate any portion of the First system he is to be driven out by immediate local counter attacks.

9. Battle Zone -
(a) Should the enemy penetrate any portion of the Battle Zone he must be prevented from spreading outwards and rolling up the position.
Immediate local counter attacks will be made to recapture any portion of this zone into which the enemy may have penetrated but if these fail or cannot be delivered in time, the operation must become a regularly prepared attack including reconnaisance, artillery bombardment and all other necessary details.
Attempt of a nature half way between the two have usually proved disastrous and are not to be made.

(b) The front line of the second system must be maintained at all costs; if necessary the Reserve Brigade may be employed for this purpose. It may however be necessary to employ the Reserve Brigade in the Forward Zone. Permanent garrisons hold the following localities in the Front line Second system -

RAILWAY RESERVE .. 1 Company of Infantry.
HENIN HILL ...... 1 Company of Infantry.

PART II - continued -

10. Machine Guns -

The machine guns are grouped in pairs or batteries -

(a) for the defence of the ground between the Support and Reserve Lines First System.

(b) for the defence of the ground between the Reserve Line First System and Front line Second system.

(c) as garrisons of special localities in the Second and Third systems.

# APPENDIX I.

## Signalling arrangements -

(a) Communication from assembly positions to Brigade Headquarters - T.21.d.5.9.

**22nd N.F. Telephone -**

Messages to be handed in at Signal Office Right (103rd Inf. Bde.) Brigade, B.4.b.2.3. or Right Group R.F.A., B.4.d.4.8.

Visual direct to Brigade Headquarters.

**23rd N.F. Telephone -**

A direct line to Brigade Headquarters is being laid to-day (March 11th). Messages may also be handed in at Signal Office 207th Field Co. R.E. T.8.c.1.5.

**25th N.F. Telephone -**

A direct line is being laid to Brigade Head-:quarters to-day (March 11th).

Visual direct to Brigade Headquarters.

**102 L.T.M.B.**

Messages will be sent through Signal Office 25th N.F.

(b) Communications forward of assembly positions -

The following is a list of Signal Stations all of which will accept messages for Brigade Headquarters. In addition units will make arrangements for visual signal communication to Brigade Headquarters as necessary.

Right Brigade Area -

| | | | | | |
|---|---|---|---|---|---|
| Right Battalion | H.Q. | U.25.b.8.2. | Telephone, | visual, | wireless |
| Left Battalion.. | H.Q. | U.26.a.7.5. | " | " | " |
| Reserve Battn... | H.Q. | U.25.b.9.1. | " | " | " |

Left Brigade Area -

| | | | | |
|---|---|---|---|---|
| Right Battalion. | H.Q. | U.13.b.55.10. | Telephone, | visual. |
| Left Battalion.. | H.Q. | T.6.b.4.0. | " | " |
| Support Battn... | H.Q. | T.23.d.5.9. | " | " |

also any battery of artillery, O.P. or other signal station will accept messages for transmission to Brigade Headquarters.

34th Division

WAR
DIARY

B. H. Q.

102nd INFANTRY BRIGADE

APRIL 1918

Appendices attached:- Operation Orders.
Intelligence Summaries
3 Maps.

REFERENCE
Firing Lines
Support
Reserve
ARMY LINE
New Trenches
(Proposed or being dug)
METRES

Vol 28

# ~WAR DIARY~

## HEADQUARTERS,

## 102nd INFANTRY BRIGADE,

## APRIL 1918.

Army Form C. 2118.

# WAR DIARY
or
# ~~INTELLIGENCE SUMMARY.~~

Volume 29.

Instructions regarding War Diaries and Intelligence Summaries are contained in F. S. Regs., Part II. and the Staff Manual respectively. Title pages will be prepared in manuscript.

(Erase heading not required.)

H.Q. 102nd Infantry Brigade — April 1918

| Place | Date | Hour | Summary of Events and Information | Remarks and references to Appendices |
|---|---|---|---|---|
| ERQUINGHEM H4d.3.7. Sheet 36 | 1st | | 102nd Brigade was in Divisional Reserve in ERQUINGHEM area. | |
| | 4th | | O.O. 200 issued. | |
| B.9.b.55.00 | 5th | | 102nd Inf. Bde relieved 101st Inf Bde in Left Section 34 Div front in accordance with O.O. 200. | Appendix 1(a) |
| " | 7th | | The enemy bombarded ARMENTIERES very heavily with H.E. and large quantities of yellow cross gas shell throughout the night 7/8th April. Bombardment commenced about 8pm April 7th and continued until about 8am April 8th. Practically the whole of 2 companies 25th NF billetted in the LUNATIC ASYLUM ARMENTIERES and in NOUVEL HOUPLINES were gassed in spite of having worn box-respirators for 10 hours. | |
| " | 8th | | Gas hung about the area bombarded throughout 8th and 9th and made it dangerous for troops. 2 Cos. 15th R. Scots were placed under command of G.O.C. 102nd Inf Bde.: one of these companies was attached to 25th NF as reserve and was accommodated in the CROSS CUT on night April 8/9th, the other remained at the ERQUINGHEM LAUNDRIES as Bde. Reserve. | |
| " | 9th | | Heavy bombardment heard to the South. Reports received that enemy attacked front of Portuguese Corps and 40th Div about 9am. Front of 102nd Inf Bde remained quiet throughout the day except for intermittent shelling of NOUVEL HOUPLINES. | |
| " | " | 3pm | 2 platoons (1 from each battalion 102nd Inf Bde) at the Brigade School moved forward and occupied the line H.5.d.5.1 – southern outskirts of RUE MARLE – CROWN PRINCE HOUSE. Line prolonged to RUE ALLEE by details 25th NF. Company 15th R. Scots in Brigade Reserve at ERQUINGHEM LAUNDRIES moved to railway embankment H.6.c. | |
| | | Later | Reserve Co. 22 NF moved to LUNATIC ASYLUM I.2.a and placed under orders of O.C. 25th N.F. | |

2353 Wt. W2544/1454 700,000 5/15 D. D. & L. A.D.S.S./Forms/C. 2118.

Instructions regarding War Diaries and Intelligence Summaries are contained in F. S. Regs., Part II. and the Staff Manual respectively. Title pages will be prepared in manuscript.

# WAR DIARY

*or*

~~INTELLIGENCE SUMMARY.~~

*(Erase heading not required.)*

HQ 102 Inf. Bde  April 1918

Army Form C. 2118.

| Place | Date | Hour | Summary of Events and Information | Remarks and references to Appendices |
|---|---|---|---|---|
| B.27b.55.00. | 9th | 7-30pm | 25th NF (with attached Coy 15th R. Scots and 22 NF) made responsible for defence of the CROSS CUT in right battalion area and of the line from the CROSS CUT in CHAPELLE D'ARMENTIERES via RUE ALLEE to CROWN PRINCE HOUSE. | |
| | | | 2 German prisoners captured at C.22d.9.3 at 6.45pm | |
| " | 10th | 4am | 9th Battn. Cheshire Regt. (19th Div) arrived at NIEPPE and was placed under the orders of G.O.C. 102nd Inf Bde for use only in case of urgent necessity. | |
| | | about 6am | Enemy attacked North of R. LYS and drove back 25th Div on our left. 102nd Inf Bde front remained quiet | |
| | | 11-40am | orders received to withdraw to ESTAIRES-LYS line North of R.LYS commencing at 3pm: front to be held by 102nd Inf Bde was to be from road B29a-B28b to LA CLEF DE LA BELGIQUE | |
| | | 12-20pm | 23rd NF ordered to take over (from 22 NF) the portion of the First Battle System from SPAIN Rd. Nachinist to R. LYS | |
| | | 12.45pm | Orders received to commence withdrawal at once. | |
| | | 1-20pm | BM 186 (order for withdrawal confirming verbal instructions) issued. | |
| TROIS ROIS NIEPPE | | about 5.30pm | Bde HQ moved to TROIS ROIS, at NIEPPE. | |
| | | | About 6.30pm the whole of 102nd Inf Bde was withdrawn North of the R. LYS. By this time the enemy had penetrated East of ERQUINGHEM to the line of the BAILLEUL-ARMENTIERES railway between the R. LYS and STEENWERCK station and had crossed the railway at LE VEAU about 3pm, but was driven back about 7pm by an attack carried out by the servants, runners, signallers etc. of 102nd Inf Bde H.Q. | |

2353 Wt. W2544/1454 700,000 5/15 D. D. & L. A.D.S.S./Forms/C. 2118.

Army Form C. 2118.

# WAR DIARY
*or*
# ~~INTELLIGENCE SUMMARY.~~
*(Erase heading not required.)*

Instructions regarding War Diaries and Intelligence Summaries are contained in F. S. Regs., Part II. and the Staff Manual respectively. Title pages will be prepared in manuscript.

H.Q. 102 Inf. Bde — April 1918

| Place | Date | Hour | Summary of Events and Information | Remarks and references to Appendices |
|---|---|---|---|---|
| B.29b.55.00 | 9th | 7-30p | 25th NF (with attached Coy 15th R.S.R. and 22 NF) made responsible for defence of the CROSS CUT in right battalion area and of the line from the CROSS CUT in CHAPELLE D'ARMENTIERES via RUE ALLEE to CROWN PRINCE HOUSE. | |
| | | | 4 German prisoners captured at C22d.9.3 at 6.45p. | |
| " | 10th | 4am | A 1st Battn. Cheshire Regt. (19th Div) arrived at NIEPPE and was placed under the orders of G.O.C. 102nd Inf Bde for use only in case of urgent necessity. | |
| | | about 6am | Enemy attacked North of R. LYS and drove back 25th Div on our left. 102nd Inf Bde front remained quiet. | |
| | | 11-40a | Orders received to withdraw to ESTAIRES-LYS line North of R.LYS commencing at 3pm: front to be held by 102nd Inf Bde was to be from road B29c-B28d to LA CLEF DE LA BELGIQUE. | |
| | | 12-40p | 23rd NF ordered to take over the portion of the First Battle System from SPAIN Rd. NIEPPE to R.LYS (inserted above: "23rd NF") | |
| | | 12-45p | Orders received to commence withdrawal at once. | |
| | | 1-40p | BM 186 (order for withdrawal confirming verbal instructions) issued. | |
| TROIS ROIS NIEPPE | | about 5-30p | Bde HQ moved to TROIS ROIS at NIEPPE. | |
| | | | About 6-30p the whole of 102nd Inf Bde was withdrawn North of the R. LYS. By this time the enemy had penetrated East of ERQUINGHEM to the line of the BAILLEUL-ARMENTIERES railway between the R.LYS and STEENWERCK station and had crossed the railway at LE VEAU about 3pm but was driven back about 7pm by an attack carried out by the servants, runners, signallers etc. of 102 Inf Bde HQ | |

Instructions regarding War Diaries and Intelligence Summaries are contained in F. S. Regs., Part II. and the Staff Manual respectively. Title pages will be prepared in manuscript.

# WAR DIARY
*or*
~~INTELLIGENCE SUMMARY.~~
*(Erase heading not required.)*

Army Form C. 2118.

HQ 102 Inf Bde — April 1918

| Place | Date | Hour | Summary of Events and Information | Remarks and references to Appendices |
|---|---|---|---|---|
| S.30.a.15. | 12th | | Bde HQ moved to S.30.a.15. | |
| " | 13th | 6 am. | Enemy attacked front of 22nd NF north of DE SEULE and also 75th Inf Bde on our left at 6 am and on 3 further occasions during the morning. 22nd NF repulsed all attacks with heavy loss to the enemy and maintained their line. 75th Bde was driven back to about the line of the DE SEULE – NEUVE EGLISE road | |
| | | 3 pm | In view of the serious situation in the direction of NEUVE EGLISE four posts each held by 1 platoon. 25th NF were established in the farms T19c9.5 : T19a4.2 : S24d6.7 : S18c9.1 | |
| | | 6 pm | Enemy again attacked on the DE SEULE – BAILLEUL road and front north of it. The left of 22nd NF and 2 platoons HLI who were holding DE SEULE were slowly pressed back. | |
| | | 6-50 pm | Enemy attacked right of 75th Bde and drove them out of T19b and d. By dark the enemy had penetrated into T19b, d and c and along the DE SEULE – BAILLEUL road as far as S30d. Enemy shelled brigade and battalion HQ: a shell hit HQ 22nd NF killing Lieut. Col. STUDD his MO and other HQ officers and personnel. Bde. was ordered to withdraw: 102nd Inf Bde withdrew about 10 pm via PEUTER FARM to billets at KEERSEBROM with exception of a party of 60 men who held PEUTER FARM and the line about 150x East of it between left of 88th Inf Bde and right of 103rd Inf Bde. | |
| S4d38 | 14th | 6 am | Bde HQ moved to HILLE FARM S4d38. | |

2353 Wt. W2544/1454 700,000 5/15 D. D. & L. A.D.S.S./Forms/C. 2118.

Army Form C. 2118.

# WAR DIARY
*or*
# ~~INTELLIGENCE SUMMARY.~~
*(Erase heading not required.)*

Instructions regarding War Diaries and Intelligence Summaries are contained in F. S. Regs., Part II. and the Staff Manual respectively. Title pages will be prepared in manuscript.

HQ 102nd Inf Bde — April 1918

| Place | Date | Hour | Summary of Events and Information | Remarks and references to Appendices |
|---|---|---|---|---|
| Sud. 38. | 14th | | Enemy attacked 34 Div front: 102nd Inf Bde not engaged (except party at [illegible] FARM). | |
| | | | All attacks were repulsed | |
| | | | 102nd Inf Brigade organised as 1 composite battalion under command of Lieut. Colonel [illegible] | |
| | | | D.S.O. M.C. Strength 22 Off. 440 OR. 90 OR. 34th Bn M.G.C. attached | |
| | | | 102nd Bde ordered to and held a French line from the LUNATIC ASYLUM S 8 d to S 3 d 9 7. | |
| | | | 34 Div was relieved by 59th Div on night 14/15th. On completion of the relief 102nd Bde moved to | |
| M 33 a 6 8 | 15th | | Camp M 33 c and was in Div Reserve. Bde HQ moved to M 33 a 6 8. | |
| | | | Enemy attacked and drove in 59th Div. 102nd Bde occupied trench from S 3 c 5.6 to | |
| | | | S 3 d 7 5 at 1.45pm with 71st Inf Bde on right and 103rd Inf Bde on left. | |
| M 24 b 5 9 | 16th | | Bde HQ moved to dugouts M 24 b 5 9 at 2am. During the early morning 102nd Inf Bde was | |
| | | | withdrawn to M 33 c and S 3 a | |
| | | | 23rd NF placed under orders of G.O.C. 147th Inf Bde and moved to S 2 a. | |
| " | 17th | | 102nd Inf Bde (less 23rd NF) relieved 74th Inf Bde in the front. S 2 d 8 7 – S 3 d 3 7. | |
| | | | Lewis guns and teams of 17th [illegible] battalion were attached to 102nd Inf Bde and placed in the line. | |
| | | | 88th Inf Bde was on our left and 89th Bde on our right | |
| " | 18th | | A quiet day | |
| " | 19th | | A quiet day. Officers of 133rd French Inf Div reconnoitred the area with a view to relief. | |

Instructions regarding War Diaries and Intelligence Summaries are contained in F. S. Regs., Part II. and the Staff Manual respectively. Title pages will be prepared in manuscript.

# WAR DIARY
*or*
~~INTELLIGENCE SUMMARY.~~
*(Erase heading not required.)*

Army Form C. 2118.

HQ 102nd Inf Bde — April 1918.

| Place | Date | Hour | Summary of Events and Information | Remarks and references to Appendices |
|---|---|---|---|---|
| A29 b 5.9 | 20th | | A quiet day. OC 20? ceased. 102nd Inf Bde was relieved by 32nd Battn. 2?? ~~[illegible]~~ French Inf Regt. On relief 102nd Inf Bde assembled at PUDEFORT FARM and was reconstituted as 3 battalions and LTMB | |
| A24 d 8.9 Sheet 27 | 21st | | Bde HQ moved to A? d 8.9 at ?am. Units marched to billets as follows:– 22 NF L33d; 23 NF L3a; 25 NF L32c; 102 LTMB L3a. | |
| " | 22nd | | 102nd Inf Bde marched to ROAD CAMP F25c. | |
| L16 a 9.9 | | | Bde HQ opened at L16 a 9.9 at 12 noon | |
| " | 23rd | | 102nd Inf Bde paraded at 12 noon and was addressed by G.O.C. 34th Div. | |
| | 24th | | Training commenced. | |
| | 25th | | 25th NF employed digging POPERINGHE line. | |
| | 26th | | 102nd Inf Bde marched to POPERINGHE line and worked on portion between A28 d 7.2 and A16 b 5.7 (Sheet 28). Advanced Bde HQ established at PESEL HOEK A30d 4.2. | |
| A30d 4.2 | | | During the evening 102nd Inf Bde took over the portion of the POPERINGHE line between G20b 5.2 and the POPERINGHE - YPRES road – 25th NF on right, 23 NF in the centre, 22nd NF on the left. | |
| | " | | Bde HQ opened at L?? at midnight | |
| L12 c 0.2 | 27th | | 102nd Inf Bde relieved troops 103rd Inf Bde in BRANDHOEK line between the DRIEGOTEN BEEK and the POPERINGHE - YPRES road. Disposition:– 23rd NF on right from DRIEGOTEN BEEK to road at G12 d 6.3 inclusive; 22nd NF on left from road G12 d 6.3 to POPERINGHE - YPRES road | |

2353 Wt. W2544/1454 700,000 5/15 D. D. & L. A.D.S.S./Forms/C. 2118.

Instructions regarding War Diaries and Intelligence Summaries are contained in F. S. Regs., Part II. and the Staff Manual respectively. Title pages will be prepared in manuscript.

# WAR DIARY
*or*
# ~~INTELLIGENCE SUMMARY.~~

*(Erase heading not required.)*

HQ 102nd Inf Bde — April 1918.

Army Form C. 2118.

| Place | Date | Hour | Summary of Events and Information | Remarks and references to Appendices |
|---|---|---|---|---|
| L.12.c.0.2. | 27th | | Both [illegible]. 25th NF in reserve in POPERINGHE line between G.14.b.9.0 and the POPERINGHE YPRES road. 102 LTMB HQ G.14.a.8.9. One mortar attached [illegible] battalion. No 2 Co 34 Bn MGC attached to 102nd Inf Bde had 4 guns in position in BRANDHOEK line, 8 in POPERINGHE line and 4 in reserve. | |
| | 28th | | Intermittent [illegible] shelling of back areas. Work on POPERINGHE and BRANDHOEK lines continued | |
| | 29th | | Consistent shelling of back areas with guns and howitzers of large calibre all day. Work on trenches continued | |
| | 30th | | A quiet day. Work continued. | |

[signature] Lieut Col
Comdg 102 Inf Bde.

2353 Wt. W2544/1454 700,000 5/15 D. D. & L. A.D.S.S./Forms/C. 2118.

# CASUALTIES FOR THE MONTH OF APRIL 1918.

| UNIT. | KILLED. | | WOUNDED. | | MISSING. | | TOTAL. | |
|---|---|---|---|---|---|---|---|---|
| | Offrs. | O.R. | Offrs. | O.R. | Offrs. | O.R. | Offrs. | O.R. |
| 22nd Bn. North'd. Fus. | 5 | 3 | 12 | 16 | 3 | 440 | 20 | 459 |
| 23rd Bn. North'd. Fus. | 1 | 1 | 3 | 29 | 9 | 460 | 13 | 490 |
| 25th Bn. North'd. Fus. | 1 | 7 | 17 | 313 | - | 210 | 18 | 530 |
| 102nd T.M.Battery. | - | 1 | 1 | 16 | - | - | 1 | 17 |
| | 7 | 12 | 33 | 374 | 12 | 1110 | 52 | 1496 |

# HONOURS & AWARDS. - APRIL 1918.

N I L.

# Appendices to War Diary

# Headquarters

# 102nd Infantry Brigade

# April 1918.

SECRET

Copy No .. 15

Ref. Map
CROIX DU BAC
Sheet 1:20,000

# 102nd INFANTRY BRIGADE ORDER No.. 200

4-4-1918.

1.. The 102nd Infantry will relieve 101st Infantry Brigade in the Left Section 34th Divisional front on the night April 5th/6th in accordance with the attached Table 'A'.

2.. All moves will be by parties not greater than platoons at not less than 200 yards distance.

3.. Anti-aircraft Lewis gun positions are to be relieved during daylight on April 5th.

4.. Signal personnel will be relieved by 5 p.m. April 5th.

5.. Units will take over from Units 101st Infantry Brigade to be relieved all Defence Schemes, trench maps, aeroplane photographs, intelligence about the enemy, details of work in hand and proposed, all S.A.A. grenades, rations, water and all other trench stores.

Each Unit will send advance parties to arrive at the H.Q. of the Unit 101st Infantry Brigade to be relieved at 4 p.m. to take over trench stores, etc. during daylight.

Units 102nd Infantry Brigade will hand over to Units 101st Infantry Brigade respectively the Provisional Defence Scheme, Reserve Brigade, 34th Division, and all area and billet stores.

Lists of stores taken over and handed over will be forwarded by each Unit to Brigade Headquarters by 9 p.m. April 6th.

Units will also take over copies of the following letters issued by 101st Infantry Brigade :-

B.M. 15/108 (method of dealing with hostile T.M's)
B.M.11/64 (method of holding front & support lines)
B.M. 60/9 (instructions regarding artillery liason Officers)
B.M.2/120 and B.M.2/121 (instructions regarding astillery action in case of S.S.O. & Artillery notes)

6.. No transport will proceed East of ST. VAAST Church, C.25.d.3.7. before 8 p.m.

7.. Units 101st Infantry Brigade are providing guides for Units 102nd Infantry Brigade at the rate of one per platoon for front line companies and one per company for companies in Support and Reserve.

8.. Advance parties of units 101st Infantry Brigade are to arrive at the H.Q. of Units 102nd Infantry Brigade at 3 p.m. April 5th to take over billets in the ERQUINGHEM area.

9.. All other details of relief will be arranged direct between C.O's concerned.

10.. Completion of reliefs will be reported to Brigade Headquarters by telegraphing the word SALMON.

11.. G.O.C. 102nd Infantry Brigade will assume command of the Left Section, 34th Divisional front on completion of the relief.

12.. 102nd Infantry Brigade Headquarters will close at ERQUINGHEM at 4 p.m. April 5th and re-open at the JUTE FACTORY, B.29.b.55. . at the same hour.

ACKNOWLEDGE.

H. L. Bridge
Major.
BRIGADE MAJOR.
102nd INFANTRY BRIGADE.

102 B.H.Q.

Issued at 8 p.m. to -

| | |
|---|---|
| G.O.C. ................ | Copy No. 1 |
| Brigade Major .......... | " 2 |
| Staff Captain .......... | " 3 |
| Signals ................ | " 4 |
| Bde. Transport Officer . | " 5 |
| 22nd N.F. .............. | " 6 |
| 23rd N.F. .............. | " 7 |
| 25th N.F. .............. | " 8 |
| 102nd T.M.B. ........... | " 9 |
| 34th Division .......... | " 10 |
| 101st Infantry Brigade .. | " 11 |
| 103rd Infantry Brigade . | " 12 |
| 102nd Bde. Supply Officer | " 13 |
| 102nd Field Ambulance .. | " 14 |

--

Diary and File .......... Copies Nos. 15 & 1[illegible]

R E L I E F on APRIB 5/6th 1918. TABLE "A". To accompany 103 Inf. Bde. Order No. 200

| Serial No. | UNIT | Relieves | In | Guides | | Hand over billets to | R E M A R K S. |
|---|---|---|---|---|---|---|---|
| | | | | Rendezvous | Time head of unit to arrive | | |
| 1 | 103 L.T.M.B. | 101 L.T.M.B. | Line | To be arranged by O.C's Batteries. | | 101 L.T.M.B. | The 3 mortars in rear positions to be relieved by 4.0 p.m.: the 2 in forward positions immediately after dark. |
| 2 | 22nd N.F. | 11th SUFFOLKS. | Left Subsector. | Level crossing NOUVELLES HOUPLINES C.27.a.20.12. | 8.0 p.m. | 13th R. SCOTS. | |
| 3 | 25th N.F. | 15th R. SCOTS | Right Subsector | Level Crossing H.3.a.05.90 | 7.30 p.m. | 15th R. SCOTS | To march from ERQUINGHEM in rear of 22nd N.F. |
| 4 | 23rd N.F. | 16th R. SCOTS | Central Subsector | Level Crossing NOUVELLE HOUPLINES C.27.a.20.12 | 9.0 p.m. | 11th SUFFOLKS | To march from ERQUINGHEM in rear of 25th Bn. N.F. |

S E C R E T

Copy No ... 14

# 102nd INFANTRY BRIGADE PROVISIONAL DEFENCE SCHEME

## LEFT SUB-SECTOR 34th DIVISIONAL FRONT.

Ref. Map Sheets 27 NE & 28 NW 1:20,000

1.. The VIIIth Corps, of which 34th Division forms a part, is organising for defence systems of trenches in rear of those in which other Corps in the line are operating.

SYSTEMS OF DEFENCE - 2.. The different systems of defence in and near the 34th Divisional area are -

(a) the BRANDHOEK system

(b) the POPERINGHE system

(c) the RENINGHELST system, a switch line facing South which runs approximately Westwards from GOEDMOET MILL G.30.b.

(d) the ABEELE system, a switch line which runs approximately Westwards from the EAST POPERINGHE line at G.14.d.8.6.

(e) There is also another switch, at present unnamed on the general line of the light railway in G.23.c., G.22., G.21., G.26. and G.25.

3.. The BRANDHOEK system consists of -

(a) a piquet line

(b) a front line breastwork

(c) a support line breastwork

(d) communication trenches between the front and support lines.

4.. The EAST POPERINGHE system consists of -

(a) a piquet line

(b) a front line trench

(c) a support line trench

(d) a reserve line trench

(e) defended localities between the support and reserve lines, that in G.14.b. known as G, that in G.9.c. as H and that in G.9.a. as I.

BOUNDARIES - 5.. (a) The 34th Divisional area is bounded on the South by the line GOEDMOET MILL G.30.b.9.4. - road junction G.23.c.6.5. - junction of railway & POPERINGHE line G.26.b.6.9. all exclusive.

(b) The Northern boundary of 34th Divisional area is the POPERINGHE - YPRES road exclusive.

INTER BRIGADE BOUNDARIES - 6..

INTER BRIGADE BOUNDARIES - 6.. The 34th Divisional Area is sub-divided into 2 Sub-sectors :-
dividing line between sub-sectors is DRIBOMBEEK (G.18.d.2.3.) - road junction G.17.c.6.9. - road junction G.14.d.9.9. all inclusive to Right Sub-sector.

METHOD OF HOLDING THE LINE - 7.. The 101st Infantry Brigade is at present holding the Right Sub-sector, 102nd Infantry Brigade the Left Sub-sector 103rd Infantry Brigade is in Divisional Reserve in Camps about L.7. 8 & 14.

ORGANISATION OF LEFT SUB-SECTOR - 8.. One Infantry battalion of 102nd Infantry Brigade is allotted for the defence of the BRANDHOEK system.
One Infantry battalion of 102nd Infantry Brigade is allotted for the defence of -

(a) all posts which are to be constructed between the Support Line of the BRANDHOEK system and the POPERINGHE system.

(b) the piquet, front and support lines of the POPERINGHE system.

One Infantry battalion 102nd Infantry Brigade in Brigade Reserve is accomodated at present, 1 Company in each of the three defended localities G, H & I, and 1 Company in the Reserve Line of the POPERINGHE system in the Left Sub-sector.
For dispositions see Map A attached.

STOKES MORTARS - 9.. 3 mortars are at present in position in the BRANDHOEK system, 1 in the POPERINGHE system and 4 in Reserve. These Stokes mortars come under the tactical orders of the O.C. battalion in whose area they are.

MACHINE GUNS - 10.. One Company of the Machine Gun Battalion is allotted to the Left Sub-sector and is disposed as follows :-

4 guns in the BRANDHOEK system

4 guns in selected positions between the BRANDHOEK ~~syste~~ and POPERINGHE systems

4 guns in the POPERINGHE system

4 guns in Divisional Reserve in L.16.a. These guns are, however, at the call of the Brigade Commander, Left Subsector.

For positions of emplacements, alternative positions and main lines of direct fire see Map A attached.

FUNCTIONS OF THE LINES OF DEFENCE & POLICY OF WORK - 11.. (a) The piquet lines in both the BRANDHOEK & POPERINGHE systems are designed -

(i) to give observation to the front where this is not possible from the front line trench.

(ii) to give warning of any hostile advance.

(iii) to break up any hostile attack before it can fully develop. For this purpose it is important that all piquets and wire and other obstacles be carefully concealed so that they may come as a surprise to the enemy .

The piquets ..

Para. 11 (continued)

The piquets of the POPERINGHE system are to be increased in size and number and will be strongly held.
The farms at H.11.a.3.3. and about L.17.c.8.8. are to be put in a state of defence and held as advanced posts, to the POPERINGHE system. In the event of a threatened hostile attack they will each be garrisoned by 1 platoon under an Officer of the battalion in the POPERINGHE line.

(b) The front line trenches of both systems are the main lines of resistance.

ACTION IN CASE OF HOSTILE ATTACK. 12.. (a) The troops in the BRANDHOEK and POPERINGHE systems including the garrisons of the outpost lines will hild their ground.

O.C's battalions holding these systems will use their reserve companies to maintain these systems respectively. This will entail delivering immediate local counter attacks by the Reserve Company or such part of it as may be necessary to regain any piquet or piquets in the outpost line which may have fallen or any other portion of the systems which may have been penetrated on their battalion front except in the case of a heavy hostile attack involving the whole line in which case O.C's battalions concerned will concentrate all their resources on maintaining the front line trench of the systems for which they are respectively responsible, the question of restoring the piquet line be referred to Brigade Headquarters.

O.C's battalions holding the BRANDHOEK and POPERINGHE Lines will cause all Officers and N.C.O's of their respective reserve Companies to carry out reconnaissances so as to be prepared to deliver local counter attacks at short notice to regain any piquets or portion of the front trench which may have been temporarily lost. In studying the ground during these reconnaissances Officers should bear in mind the value of flank attacks upon an enemy when held up in a pocket and the co-operation of Stokes mortars, rifle grenades, Vickers and Lewis guns. They must not always depend on artillery support.

(b) The action of the Battalion in Brigade Reserve will depend largely on the direction and progress of the hostile attack.

This battalion will carry out reconnaissances so as to be prepared for any of the following alternatives:

(i) to reinforce the BRANDHOEK system

(ii) to form a defensive flank to the South. A possible line in this connection might be that of the BUSSBOOM - VLAMERTINGHE road which includes the prominent knoll on which LINDE GOED FARM is situated.

(iii) to form a defensive flank to the North along the general line of the POPERINGHE - YPRES road from about G.3.d. to BRANDHOEK line.

(iv) to counter attack with either the whole or part of the battalion as the situation may require either or both of the defended posts in L.11.a. and L.17.c.

Para. 12 (continued)

(v) to counter attack on the whole or part of the BRANDHOEK system in the Left Sub-sector.

In the event of any of the above alternatives being ordered minimum garrisons of 1 platoon will be left in each of the defended localities G H & I until relieved.

HEAD-QUARTERS - 13.. In the event of it being necessary to fight the BRANDHOEK Line an Advanced Report Centre will be established at G.16.d.5.7. to which place all reports will be sent. The time at which this Report Centre will open will be notified to all concerned.

Major.
BRIGADE MAJOR.
5-8-1918 102nd INFANTRY BRIGADE.

DISTRIBUTION -

| | | |
|---|---|---|
| G.O.C. ............. | Copy No. | 1 |
| Brigade Major ..... | " | 2 |
| Staff Captain ..... | " | 3 |
| Signals ........... | " | 4 |
| 22nd N.F. ......... | " | 5 |
| 23rd N.F. ......... | " | 6 |
| 25th N.F. ......... | " | 7 |
| 102 L.T.M.S. ...... | " | 8 |
| No. 2 Coy. 34th Bn. M.G.C. ...... | " | 9 |
| 34th Division ..... | " | 10 |
| 101 Inf. Bde ...... | " | 11 |
| 103 Inf. Bde ...... | " | 12 |
| 208th Fld.Coy. R.E. | " | 13 |
| Diary & file ...... | " | 14 & 15 |

SECRET.

Copy No. 9

102ND INFANTRY BRIGADE ORDER NO. 201.

Ref. Maps.
Sheets 27 N.E.
28 S.W. - 1:20,000
& Sheet 27 - 1:40,000.

20-4-18

1. The 34th Division is to be relieved by the 133rd French Division to-night.

2. The 102nd Infantry Brigade will be relieved by the 3rd Battalion 401st French Infantry Regiment.
The leading troops 401st French Infantry Regiment are due to arrive at the Road Junction [illegible] at midnight. The leading Company will march by the road leading South through S.8.b. and will relieve the Right of the 102nd Infantry Brigade. The next Company will march by the main road from [illegible] to the Road Junction S.3.d.5.7. and will relieve the left of the 102nd Infantry Brigade and a portion of the 49th Infantry Brigade.
The 3rd Company will relieve the troops of the 102nd Infantry Brigade in the First Army line.

3. Guides to lead the 3rd Battalion 401st French Infantry Regiment as far as the Road Junction [illegible] are being provided under Brigade arrangements. O.C. 102 Brigade Composite Battalion will detail guides to meet the 3rd Battalion 401st French Infantry Regt. at the Road Junction [illegible] and lead them to the trenches.

4. All Vickers Gunners of 34th and 49th Divisions and all Lewis Gun detachments of 12th Tank Battalion will withdraw from the line with the Companies in whose area they now are and will march with them as far as the assembly position mentioned in para. 7, after which they will march independently to the Road Junction at ST. [illegible] where they will come under the orders of O.C. 34th Battalion M.G.C. and O.C. 12th Tank Battalion respectively.
Transport for the conveyance of the above Vickers guns is being arranged by O.C. 34th Battalion M.G.C. and will be formed up at 1.30 a.m. facing North on the [illegible] Road head at Road Junction [illegible]. No transport is available to carry the Lewis Guns of 12th Tank Battalion.

5. O.C. 102 Bde. Composite Battalion will detail special parties from his reserves to collect immediately after dusk and dump at his Headquarters all reserve S.A.A. and Stokes Mortar ammunition and one tool per man of his composite battalion. A loading party under an Officer will be left in charge of this dump.
The Brigade Transport Officer will detail 4 G.S. Wagons to report to the Officer in charge of the loading party at Battalion Headquarters, [illegible], at 2.0 a.m. All tools and as much S.A.A. as possible will be loaded on to these wagons and taken to the assembly position mentioned in para. 7. The loading party will proceed to the assembly position as soon as the wagons have been loaded.

6.. The Brigade Transport Officer will detail 4 L.G.S. wagons to be formed up at 8.0 a.m. on the CROIX DE POPERINGHE -- MONT NOIR Road facing North immediately in rear of transport 25th Battalion N.F. for conveyance of Lewis Guns and Magazines and Stokes Mortars of units 102nd Infantry Brigade. When loaded these wagons will proceed to the assembly position.

7.. On relief all troops 102nd Infantry Brigade will march to a position of assembly about R.22.d. where they will be met by an Officer of the Brigade Staff who will allot assembly areas. Guides are being provided under Brigade arrangements and will be stationed at the Cross Roads R.30.a.0.7 to conduct troops to the assembly area. The Brigade Transport Officer will arrange for cookers with hot food to be at the assembly position at 5.0 a.m.

8... On arrival at the assembly position the 102nd Brigade Composite Battalion will be broken up and the 102nd Infantry Brigade re-organised into 3 battalions and L.T.M.B. as normally.
For the present the 102 L.T.M.B. will be attached to the 23rd N.F.

9... The 102nd Infantry Brigade will continue the march to R.3.a. and L.33.d. on the morning of April 21st. Orders for this move will be issued later.

10... Completion of relief will be reported to Brigade Headquarters.

11... Brigade Headquarters will close at MONT NOIR on completion of the relief and reopen at the assembly position in R.22.d. at the same hour.

ACKNOWLEDGE.

[signature]
Major.
BRIGADE MAJOR.
102nd INFANTRY BRIGADE.

Issued at 6.0 p.m. to -

G.O.C. ..... Copy No. 1
Brigade Major " " 2
Staff Captain " " 3
Signals " " 4
Bde. Transport Off. " 5
102 Bde. Composite Bn. " 6, 7, 8, 9, & 10.
34th Division. " 11
88th Bde. 12
89th Bde. 13
34th Bn. M. G. C. 14
17th Tank Battalion. 15
No. 3 Coy. Div. Train 16.
401st French Inf. Regt..... 17.

SECRET. Copy No. 10

Ref. Map
Sheet 27
1:40,000.

102nd INFANTRY BRIGADE ORDER No.. 202

21:4:1918.

1. The 102nd Brigade Group will march to-morrow, April 22nd, to the ST. JAN-ter-BIEZEN area in accordance with the attached table.

2. The following distances will be maintained on the line of march :-

Between Companies .. 100x
Between Battalions .. 500x
Between each unit and its transport .. 100x

In addition gaps of 25x will be left between each Section of 6 vehicles.

Transport will march with units.

The usual halts will be observed.

3. Billetting parties at the rate of 1 Officer and 3 N.C.O's, (includes 1 for transport), per Infantry Battalion will report to the Staff Captain outside the office of the Area Commandant ST. JAN-ter-BIEZEN at 11.0 a.m. April 22nd.

4. Arrival in billets and position of Headquarters will be reported by each unit to Brigade Headquarters.

5. Brigade Headquarters will close at BOESCHEPPE at 10.0 a.m. and reopen at ST.JAN-ter-BIEZEN at the same hour.

ACKNOWLEDGE.

Major.
BRIGADE MAJOR.
102nd INFANTRY BRIGADE.

21:4:1918.
Issued at 9.30 p.m. to -

G.O.C. ..... Copy No. 1
Brigade Major " " 2
Staff Captain " " 3
Signals .... " " 4
Bde. Transport Off. " 5
22nd N.F. ......... " 6
23rd N.F. ... " 7
25th N.F. ... " 8

102 L.T.M.B. .. Copy No. 9
H.Q. 34th Div.. " " 10
34th Bn. M.G.C. " " 11
~~O.C. 34th Div. Train " 12~~
O.C. No. 3 Coy. Div. Train 13
-----
War Diary and File .. 14 & 15

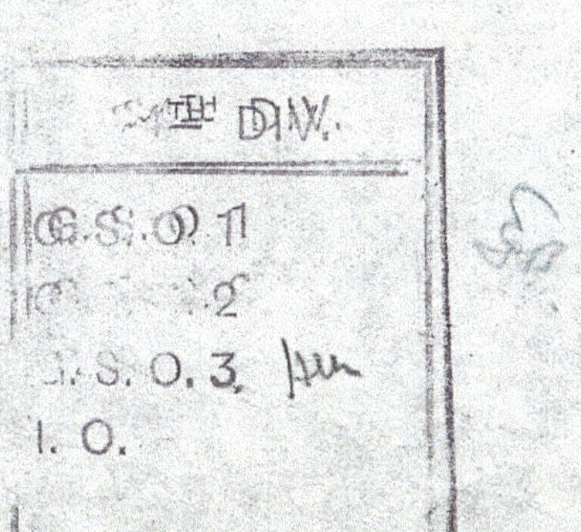

MARCH TABLE. APRIL 22nd 1918.

To accompany O.O. No.. 202.

| Serial No. | UNIT | STARTING POINT | | ROUTE | DESTINATION |
|---|---|---|---|---|---|
| | | Place | Time to pass | | |
| 1 | 22nd N.F. | Railway Crossing L.32.b.8.4. | 10 a.m. | ABEELE - - Cross Roads K.24.b.9.0. - Cross Roads K.17.b.6.8. - Cross Roads L.1.d.8.1. | Road Camp No. 1 F.25.c |
| 2 | 25th N.F. | - ditto - | 10.15 am | - ditto - | -dittoe |
| 3 | 23rd N.F. | - ditto - | 10.30 a.m. | - ditto - | -ditto- |
| 4 | 102nd LTMB | - ditto - | 10.45 a.m. | - ditto - | -ditto- |
| 5 | Bde. H.Q.... | - ditto - | 10.46 a.m. | - ditto - | ST. JAN-ter-BIEZEN. |
| 6 | 34th Bn. M.G. C.. | -ditto- | 11.5 a.m. | - ditto - | Road Camp No.. 1 F.25.c. |

SECRET. Copy No. [illegible]

Ref. Map
Sheet 27
1:40,000.

102nd INFANTRY BRIGADE ORDER No. 209

21:4:1918.

1. The 102nd Brigade group will march to-morrow, April 22nd, to the ST. JANS-ter-BIEZEN area in accordance with the attached table.

2. The following distances will be maintained on the line of march :-

Between Companies .. 100x
Between Battalions .. 200x
Between each unit and its transport .. 100x

In addition gaps of 25x will be left between each Section of 6 vehicles.

Transport will march with units.

The usual halts will be observed.

3. Billeting parties at the rate of 1 Officer and 2 N.C.O's, (includes 1 for transport) per Infantry Battalion will report to the Staff Captain outside the office of the Area Commandant ST. JANS-ter-BIEZEN at 11.0 a.m. April 22nd.

4. Arrival in billets and position of Headquarters will be reported by each unit to Brigade Headquarters.

5. Brigade Headquarters will close at [illegible] at 10.0 a.m. and reopen at ST.JANS-ter-BIEZEN at the same hour.

ACKNOWLEDGE.

[signature illegible]
Major.
BRIGADE MAJOR.
102nd INFANTRY BRIGADE.

21:4:1918.
Issued at 9.30 p.m. to -

| | | | | | |
|---|---|---|---|---|---|
| G.O.C. ..... | Copy No. 1 | | 102 L.T.M.B. .. | Copy No. 9 |
| Brigade Major | " " 2 | | R.A. 34th Div.. | " " 10 |
| Staff Captain | " " 3 | | 34th Bn. M.G.C. | " " 11 |
| Signals .... | " " 4 | | ~~[illegible]~~ | ~~" " 12~~ |
| Bde. Transport Off. | " " 5 | | O.C. No. 2 Coy. Div. Train | 13 |
| 22nd N.F. ......... | " " 6 | | | |
| 23rd N.F. ... | " " 7 | | | |
| 25th N.F. ... | " " 8 | | War Diary and File .. | 14 & 15 |

MARCH TABLE. APRIL 22nd 1918.

To accompany O.O. No.. 206.

| Serial No. | UNIT | STARTING POINT | | ROUTE | DESTINATION |
|---|---|---|---|---|---|
| | | Place | Time to Pass | | |
| 1 | 22nd N.F. | Railway Crossing L.22.b.6.4. | 10 a.m. | ABEELE – Cross Roads L.34.b.8.0. – Cross Roads K.17.b.4.2. – Cross Roads L.1.a.8.1. | Road Camp No. 1 F.26.c |
| 2 | 20th N.F. | – ditto – | 10.10 am | – ditto – | –ditto– |
| 3 | 23rd N.F. | – ditto – | 10.20 a.m. | – ditto – | –ditto– |
| 4 | 102nd L.T.M.B. | – ditto – | 10.30 a.m. | – ditto – | –ditto– |
| 5 | Bde. H. .... | – ditto – | 10.35 a.m. | – ditto – | CP. JAN-TER-BIEZEN. |
| 6 | 34th Bn. M.G. C.. | –ditto– | 11.0 a.m. | – ditto – | Road Camp No.. 1 F.26.c. |

SECRET

Ref. Maps
Sheets 27 &
28 1:40,000
Sheet 28 N.W.
1:20,000

Copy No ... 17

# 102nd INFANTRY BRIGADE ORDER No. 205

23-4-1918

1.. Unless orders are previously issued to the contrary, 102nd Brigade Group will march this morning in accordance with attached Table 'A' and work on the portion of the Army Line N.E. of POPERINGHE between G.4.b.5.9. and A.16.b.1.7.

2.. First line transport together with cookers and water carts will accompany all Units of the Group.

Remainder of transport will remain in its present position.

Lewis gun limbers will march immediately in rear of their battalion: all other first line transport of the Group will march in rear of the column in order of march of Units and under the Brigade Transport Officer.

3.. Distances of 200 yards will be maintained between Companies and between the transport of each Unit of the Group on the march.

4.. On arrival at the Army line, 25th N.F. will work on the right, 23rd N.F. on the centre and 22nd N.F. on the left sections respectively.

O.C. 208th Field Coy. R.E. is proceeding ahead of the column to reconnoitre the work and is arranging for guides to meet units at A.28.c.4.7. on the POPERINGHE - ELVERDINGHE road and lead them to their work.

5.. Packs and blankets will be collected ready for loading on to transport should orders be issued for them to be sent up to the line.

6.. O.C. No. 2 Coy. 34th Bn. M.G.C. will reconnoitre positions for machine guns to cover the 102nd Brigade sector of the Army line (vide para. 1).

7.. It is possible that during the course of the day the 34th Division may be ordered to carry out any of the following alternatives :-

(a) to man the line which is being dug.

(b) to assist the XXII Corps in the direction of DICKEBUSCH.

(c) to assist the II Corps on the line BOESINGHE - YPRES.

(d) to assist the Belgian Army on the canal line N of BOESINGHE.

In the event of the 102nd Brigade being ordered to man the line, battalions will hold the sections which have been allotted to them to dig.

8.. An Advanced Brigade Headquarters will be established about A.21. on completion of the march: the exact position will be notified later. All reports will be sent to this Advanced H.Q. The office of the Staff Captain will remain in its present position at ST. JAN TER BIEZEN.

ACKNOWLEDGE

[signature]

Major.
BRIGADE MAJOR.
102nd INFANTRY BRIGADE.

Issued at 2 a.m. to -

| | | |
|---|---|---|
| G.O.C. .................. | Copy No. 1 | |
| Brigade Major ........... | " 2 | |
| Staff Captain ........... | " 3 | |
| Signals ................. | " 4 | |
| Bde. Transport Officer .. | " 5 | |
| 22nd N.F. ............... | " 6 | |
| 23rd N.F. ............... | " 7 | |
| 25th N.F. ............... | " 8 | |
| 102 L.T.M.B. ............ | " 9 | |
| 208th Fld. Coy. R.E. ... | " 10 | |
| No. 2 Coy. 34th Bn. M.G.C | " 11 | |
| 34th Division. .......... | " 12 | for information. |
| 103rd Inf. Bde. ......... | " 13 | for information. |
| No. 3 Coy. Div. Train ... | " 14 | for information. |
| 102nd Field Ambulance ... | " 15 | for information. |
| Area Commandant, ST. JAN TER BIEZEN. | " 16 | |
| War Diary & File ........ | " 17 & 18 | |

Table 'A' To accompany 102nd Inf. Bde. Order No... 203

March on April 26th.

| Serial No. | Troops in order of march. | Starting Point Place | Starting Point Time to pass | ROUTE | Destination | REMARKS |
|---|---|---|---|---|---|---|
| 1 | 1 Co. 22nd N.F. | Road junction ST.JAN TER BIEZEN L.2.a.4.7. | 8.15 a.m. | Cross roads L.4.b. thence switch road N. of POPERINGHE to G.3.a.2.0. thence along ELVERDINGHE rd. | Left Section | Will act as advanced guard to Bde. Group after road junct. L.4.b. |
| 2 | 208th Field Coy. R.E. | - do - | 8.18 a.m. | - do - | 102 Bde. Sector of Army line. | |
| 3 | 22nd N.F. less 1 Company. | - do - | 8.22 a.m. | - do - | Left Section. | |
| 4 | Brigade H.Q. & 102 L.T.M.B. | - do - | 8.34 a.m. | - do - | About G.21. | |
| 5 | 23rd N.F. | - do - | 8.37 a.m. | - do - | Centre Section. | |
| 6 | 25th N.F. | - do - | 9.2 a.m. | - do - | Right Section. | |
| 7 | No. 2 Coy. 34th Bn. M.G.C. | - do - | 9.17 a.m. | To as far as G.2.a.6.7. thence along WOESTEN road | Position of assembly about A.21.c.8.1 | |
| 8 | 1st line transport of all Units (less Lewis gun limbers | - do - | 9.25 a.m. | - do - | To be selected by Bde.TO about A.20.b. or A.21.a. | |

NOTE - Provided the tactical situation permits, the usual halts at 10 minutes to each clock hour will be observed.

SECRET
Ref Maps
Sheet 27 NE
and 28 NW
1:20,000

102nd INFANTRY BRIGADE ORDER No. 204.

Copy No... 15

27-4-1918

1.. The 34th Division boundaries have been fixed as follows -
(a) Southern (right) boundary - GOOD HOET MILL G.30.b.9.4. - road junction G.25.c.8.5. - junction of railway and POPERINGHE Line G.26.b.6.9 all exclusive.
(b) Northern (left) boundary - the POPERINGHE - YPRES road exclusive.

2.. The front of the 34th Division in the BRANDHOEK and POPERINGHE Lines is to be held by the 101 Inf. Bde on the right and the 102 Inf. Bde. on the left. Dividing line between 101 and 102 Inf. Bdes will be the junction of the DRIEGOENBEEK G.18.d.2.5. - road junction G.17.c.8.9. - road junction G.14.d.9.9. all inclusive to the right Brigade.

The 103rd Infantry Brigade is being withdrawn on relief to SCHOOL CAMP.

The front of the 102nd Infantry Brigade in the BRANDHOEK line will be held by 23rd N.F. on the right and 22nd N.F. on the left. Dividing line between battalions : junction of BRANDHOEK LINE and road G.12.d.7.3. - road junction G.11.c.8.3. both inclusive to right battalion.

3.. The method of holding the 102nd Infantry Brigade area will be as follows -

(a) The battalions holding the BRANDHOEK line (22nd & 23rd N.F.) will each subdivide their respective fronts into three Company areas. Each of these Company areas will be held by 1 platoon, the remainder of the companies being billeted West of and within 600 yards of the BRANDHOEK Line in their respective areas ready to man the line immediately in case of threatened hostile attack. One company of each battalion will be billeted in suitable positions West of the BRANDHOEK line as battalion reserves.

(b) The Companies detailed to hold the BRANDHOEK LINE will maintain outposts in the VLAMERTINGHE line on their respective fronts relieving troops of the 103rd Infantry Brigade now in these positions unti such time as they are themselves relieved by troops of 58t Infantry Brigade 19th Division when they will be withdrawn. The right battalion will take over the outposts in the VLAMERTINGHE line between H.15.c.4.5. and about H.9.c.7.3., the left battalion thence North wards to the Brigade left boundary.

(c) 25th N.F. will be in Brigade re erve and will be billeted West and within 600 yards of the POPERINGHE line in the Brigade area ready to reinforce the BRANDHOEK line or to man the POPERINGHE LINE as may be ordered in case of hostile attack. Officers liason patrols will be maintained by this battalion at the Headquarters of each battalion holding the BRANDHOEK line.

(d) Touch must be gained and maintained in the BRANDHOEK and POPERINGHE lines on the right with troops 101 Inf. Bde. and on the left wi h troops of I Corps in the case of the BRANDHOEK line and with Troops Coy. R. in the case of the POPERINGHE line.

4.. The necessary reliefs of the troops 103rd Infantry Brigade in the BRANDHOEK and VLAMERTINGHE lines in the 102nd Brigade area will be carried out by 22nd and 23rd N.F. at once, all details being arrange direct between C.O's concerned. 25th N.F. will move at once to its billets West of the POPERINGHE line.

5..

P.T.

5.. O.C. No. 2 Coy. 34th Bn. M.G.C. will relieve the Vickers guns attached 103rd Infantry Brigade in the BRANDHOEK line in the 102nd Brigade area at once in accordance with instructions already issued to him.
The Stokes mortars 102nd L.T.M.B. now attached to each battalion will remain with them and will be placed in positions in the BRANDHOEK and POPERINGHE lines by O.C. 102 L.T.M.B. in consultation with O.C. Battalion concerned.

6.. All tools now in possession of battalions will be taken with them to their new areas. 103rd Inf. Bde.s. are handing over reserve S.A.A. etc. in the BRANDHOEK line . Lists of S.A.A. etc. taken over will be forwarded to Brigade Headquarters by 3 p.m. tomorrow.

7.. Completion of reliefs will be reported to Brigade Headquarters. Each Unit will forward a sketch of its dispositions to reach Brigade Headquarters by 12 noon tomorrow.

8.. 102nd Infantry Brigade Headquarters will remain in its present position L.12.c.0.2.

ACKNOWLEDGE.

[signature]
Major.
BRIGADE MAJOR.
102nd INFANTRY BRIGADE.

Issued a 9.30 p.m. to -

| | | |
|---|---|---|
| G.O.C. .............. | Copy No. | 1 |
| Brigade Major ...... | " | 2 |
| Staff Captain ...... | " | 3 |
| Signals ............ | " | 4 |
| Bde. Transport Officer | " | 5 |
| 22nd N.F. .......... | " | 6 |
| 23rd N.F. .......... | " | 7 |
| 25th N.F. .......... | " | 8 |
| 102 L.T.M.B. ....... | " | 9 |
| No. 2 Co. 34th Bn MGC | " | 10 |
| 34th Division ...... | " | 11 |
| 101 Inf. Bde. ...... | " | 12 |
| 103rd Inf. Bde. .... | " | 13 |
| 208th Field Coy. R.E. | " | 14 |
| Diary and file ..... | " | 15 and 16 |

CONFIDENTIAL                                                  Intel G. 2.

INTELLIGENCE SUMMARY
102nd INFANTRY BRIGADE.
From 6 am 6-4-18 - 6 am 7-4-18

OUR OPERATIONS.

Patrols -

Nine patrols were out on the Brigade front during the night and report NO MAN'S LAND to be very much water logged. No hostile patrols were seen or heard.

A patrol of 5 O.R's (22nd N.F.) left our lines at 9.15 p.m. at C.23.a.15.15. and proceeded S.E. to point C.23.a.71.11. Here they took up a position and waited. Sounds of pumping could be plainly heard coming from about C.23.c.90.80. and sounds as of revetting could also be heard. Patrol returned to our lines at C.23.a.15.15. at 10.45 p.m.

Artillery and Trench Mortars -

Our artillery was active during the night firing on enemy communications at intervals.

L.T.M's fired 20 rounds on C.29.a.90.25. CENTAUR SUPPORT & Switch with good results.

Machine Guns -

Were active at 'stand to' and at intervals during the night.

Aircraft -

Our planes were continually patrolling the front during the day. At 2 p.m. a squadron passed over our right battalion front and dropped several bombs.

ENEMY INTELLIGENCE

(a) Infantry -

No infantry activity was observed.

(b) Artillery -

Between 7.20 a.m. and 7.50 am 5 5.9's fell near SUBSIDIARY line about I.4.a.50.70. At 4 a.m. 7 77 mm. shells fell about I.5.c.50.35. At 5 p.m. 16. 5.9's fell near PORT EGAL AVENUE at about I.10.b.50.98. At 4.20 p.m. 3 77 mm. fell near I.4.a.65.80. At 4 p.m. two gas shells fell near C.26.d.35.40. Between 4.30 & 6.30 pm 40 4.2's fell in vicinity of SUBSIDIARY line about C.28.c.50.50. At 11.30 p.m. several 4.2's fell into ARMENTIERES.

Trench Mortars -

At 4.30 p.m. 3 L.T.M's fell near the junction of NEWBURN & SPAIN Avenues. 12 L.T.M. fell in vicinity of C.28.d.98.45. at 5 am. Between 9 p.m. and 1 a.m. 50 L.T.M's fell about C.22.d.81.42. and 10 rds. on C.22.d., PANAMA CANAL and WESSEX AVENUE.

Machine guns -

Machine guns were active during the night particularly at about 'stand to' and fired on our aircraft during the day.

Aircraft -

Two E. A. flew over our lines at 12.15 p.m. flying very high in the direction of HOUPLINES. At 2.15 p.m. one E.A. crossed our lines about I.4.a. coming from the direction of ARMENTIERES.

NEW WORK -

Fresh soil has been thrown up about I.11.a.60.70. New work is in progress at about D.19.a.50.10. New earth for 50 yards has been thrown up.

Miscellaneous -

A small loop hole 2' long can be seen on parapet of CENSOR Support, C.23.b.45.30.

Movement -

Visibility poor. One man seen moving along CENSOR SUPPORT in C.23.b. at 2 pm

R.W. Wilkins[?] Capt.
BRIGADE MAJOR
102nd INFANTRY BDE

7-4-18

CONFIDENTIAL. Intel G. 4

INTELLIGENCE SUMMARY.
102nd INFANTRY BRIGADE.
From 6 am 8-4-1918 – 6 am 9-4-1918

OUR OPERATIONS

Patrols –
Nine patrols were out on the Brigade front during the night but no hostile patrols were encountered and no unusual sounds were heard. At 12 midnight an Officers patrol 22nd N.F. (20 O.R's & Lewis gun) left our lines at C.17.c.50.10. and proceeded E. and reached enemy wire at about C.23.b.12.20. The wire consists of one thick belt 2' 6" high and 4 to 5 yards wide. No enemy were seen but sounds as of revetting were heard coming from trench at about C.23.b.20.20. Patrol returned to our lines at 2 a.m.

Artillery –
Our artillery was active throughout the night and fired at intervals during thew day.

Trench Mortars –
3" Stokes mortars fired 30 rounds between 10 a.m. and 2 p.m. on C.29.a.90.50.

Machine Guns –
Usual activity during the night.

Aircraft –
Active in the early part of the day.

ENEMY INTELLIGENCE.

Hostile Activity –
No enemy activity was observed.

Artillery –
The gas bombardment of ARMENTIERES ceased about 8.30 a.m. 8-4-18. Several rounds H.E. 4.2" were fired into HOUPLINES between 10 a.m. and 2 p.m. At 6.15 10 rds. 4.2" fell on PANAMA CANAL about C.22.c.40.80. At 4 a.m. enemy shelled back areas, probably hi[s] targets being the river bridges. This has been going on intermitten[tly] and is still in progress at 11 a.m., H.E., 4.2"s and 5.9's being fir[ed]

Trench Mortars –
7 M.T.M. fell near C.23.b.10.40. at 10 a.m., 5 more at 6.3[0] C.23.b.10.40. and again at 5 a.m. 2 more fell. 4 L.T.M. fell near PANAMA CANAL at 6.35 p.m.. Between 9.30 p.m. and 11 p.m. 15 L.T.M's fell near C.22.d.50.20. At 12.10 a.m. 4 L.T.M's fell on WESSEX AV. C.22.d.00.80.

Machine guns –
Usual activity during the night.

Aircraft –
Active in the early part of the day and were engaged by A.

Trench Tramway –
Just before dawn sounds were heard similar to a gas engin[e] work North of WESSEX AV, probably on CEMETERY DRIVE tramway.

Miscellaneous –
Observation poor owing to ground mist. At 1.50 p.m. 6 p[uffs] of white smoke were observed at about C.24.b.20.30. but no sounds of explosion were heard.

Movement –
About 2.30 p.m. several men were seen on parapet at I.5. and were immediately dispersed with rifle fire. At 12 noon about [illegible] men with picks and shovels moved from C.18.c.25.30. and disappear[ed] again about C.23.b.98.70. At 2.15 p.m. 7 men were seen emptying [illegible] from CELT RESERVE C.17.d.20.60.

[M]ajor
BRIGADE MA[JOR]
[102]nd INF

CROIX DU BAC
TRENCHES CORRECTED TO 4-3-18
Scale 20000
Steenwerck
Nieppe
NIEPPE SYSTEM
STEENWERCK SWITCH
Croix du Bac
Erquinghem Lys
Bac St Maur
Fleurbaix

HOUPLINES
TRENCHES CORRECTED TO 23
REFERENCE
Tilleul
Wemsen Gilde
West Hook
le Touquet
Frelinghien
l'Os a Moelle
le Bizet
Urish Avenue
le Ruage
Houplines
l'Attergette
ARMENTIERES
Nouvel Houplines
Battalion
BRIGADE
Asylum
Lunatic Lane
l'Epinette
Brune Rue
l'Aventure
le Temple
Census
Censor Drive
Irvine Drive

la Chapelled'Armentières
Wez Macquart
Premesques
la Houssoie
London Bridge
Oxford Circus
Haymarket
Rue du Bois
Rue Fleurie
Bois Blancs
Trois Fetus
Mont Rindu
Blanc Coulon
la Fleur d'Ecosse
Pear Tree Farm
Hull Road
Brick St.
Central Ave.
BOUNDARY
Scale 1:10,000
INDEX TO ADJOINING SHEETS
Ordnance Survey, October
To Radinghem
To Wavrin
To Englos
To Ennetières

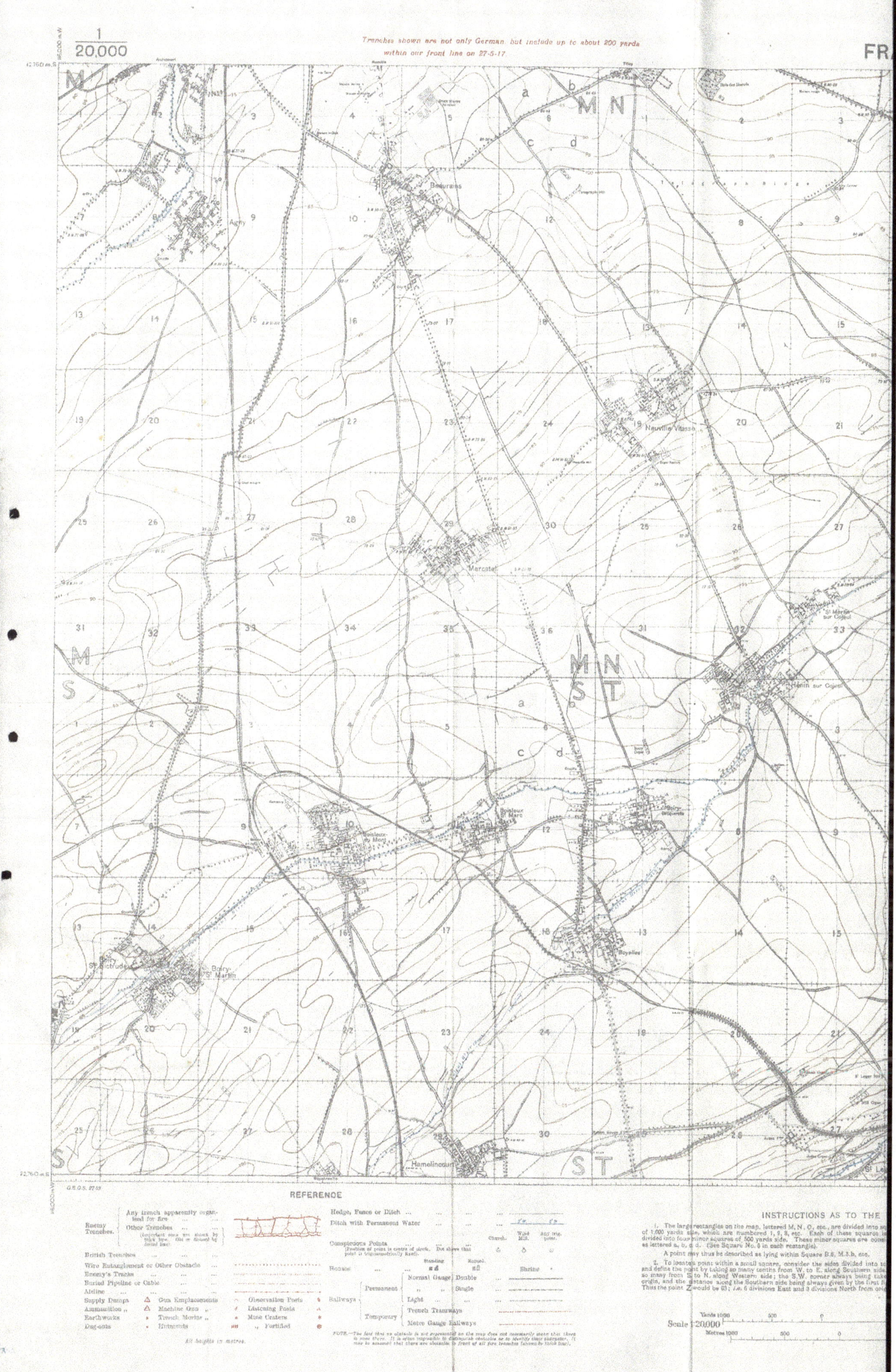
1
20,000
Trenches shown are not only German but include up to about 200 yards
within our front line on 27-5-17
FRA
Beaurains
Agny
Telegraph Ridge
Neuville Vitasse
Mercatel
St Martin sur Cojeul
Henin sur Cojeul
Boiry Becquerelle
Boisleux-au-Mont
Boisleux St Marc
Boyelles
Boiry-St Rictrude
Boiry-St Martin
Hamelincourt
G.S.G.S. 2743
REFERENCE
Enemy Trenches.
Any trench apparently organised for fire
Other Trenches
British Trenches
Wire Entanglement or Other Obstacle
Enemy's Tracks
Buried Pipeline or Cable
Airline
Supply Dumps
Ammunition „
Earthworks
Dug-outs
Gun Emplacements
Machine Gun „
Trench Mortar „
Hutments
Observation Posts
Listening Posts
Mine Craters
„ Fortified
All heights in metres.
Hedge, Fence or Ditch
Ditch with Permanent Water
Conspicuous Points
Church.
Wind Mill.
Any trig. point.
Houses
Standing
Ruined.
Shrine
Railways
Permanent
Normal Gauge
Double
Single
Light
Temporary
Trench Tramways
Metre Gauge Railways
INSTRUCTIONS AS TO THE
A point may thus be described as lying within Square B.6, M.3.b, etc.
Scale 1:20,000
Yards 1000
500
0
Metres 1000
500
0

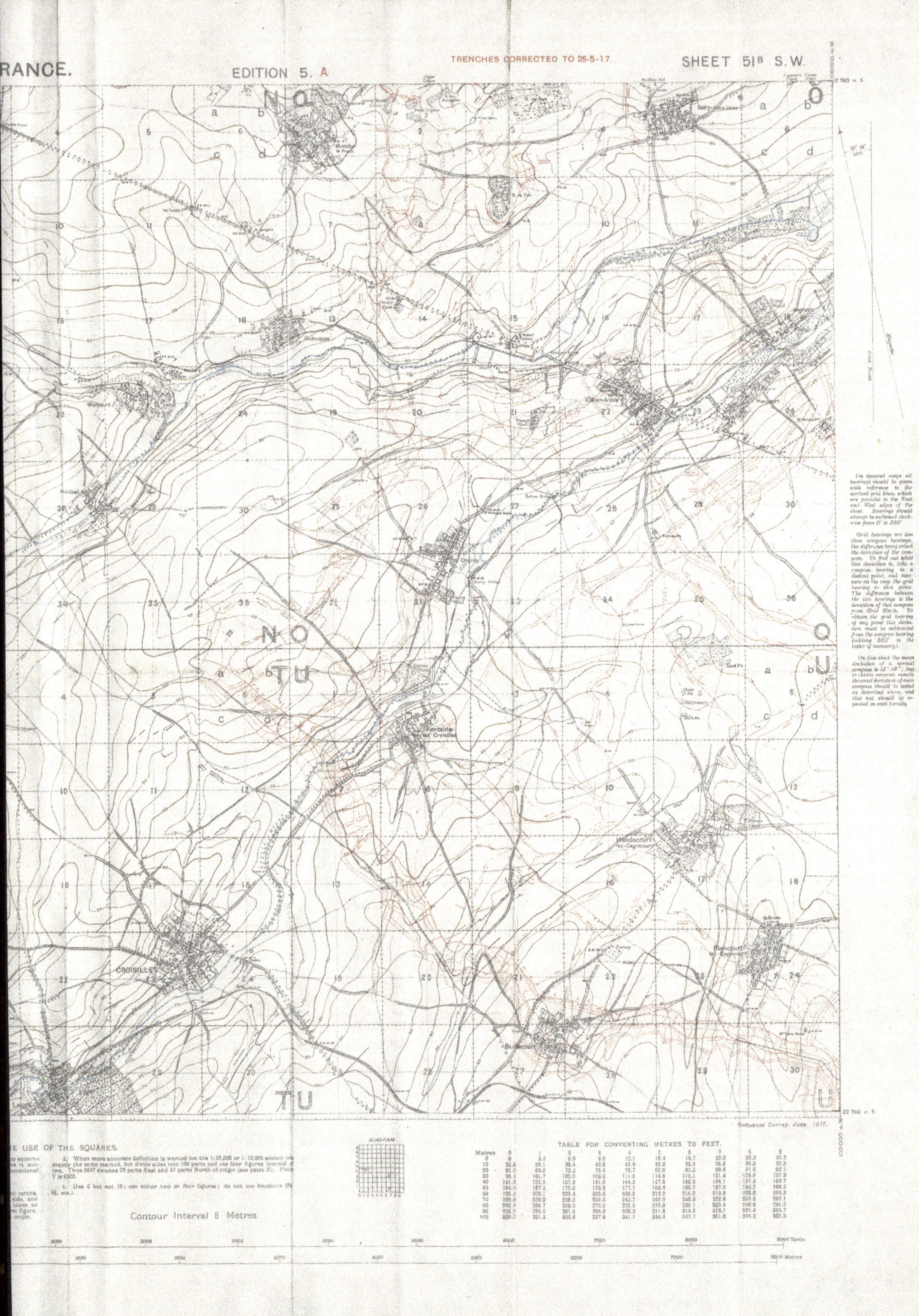

RANCE.
EDITION 5. A
TRENCHES CORRECTED TO 25-5-17.
SHEET 51B S.W.
NO
O
NO
TU
O
U
TU
U
Croisilles
Fontaine-lès-Croisilles
Hendecourt lez-Cagnicourt
Riencourt lez-Cagnicourt
Bullecourt
Vis-en-Artois
Guémappe
Wancourt
Héninel
Chérisy
Monchy le Preux
Boiry-Notre Dame
Hancourt
Sand Pit
Ordnance Survey, June, 1917.
On squared maps all bearings should be given with reference to the vertical grid lines, which are parallel to the East and West edges of the sheet. Bearings should always be reckoned clockwise from 0° to 360°.
Grid bearings are less than compass bearings, the difference being called the deviation of the compass. To find out what this deviation is, take a compass bearing to a distant point, and measure on the map the grid bearing to that point. The difference between the two bearings is the deviation of that compass from Grid North. To obtain the grid bearing of any point this deviation must be subtracted from the compass bearing (adding 360° to the latter if necessary).
On this sheet the mean deviation of a normal compass is 12° 18'; but to obtain accurate results the exact deviation of each compass should be tested as described above, and this test should be repeated in each locality.
E USE OF THE SQUARES.
3. When more accurate definition is wanted (on the 1:20,000 or 1:10,000 scales) use exactly the same method, but divide sides into 100 parts and use four figures instead of two. Thus 0847 denotes 08 parts East and 47 parts North of origin (see point X). Point Y is 6503.
4. Use 0 but not 10; use either two or four figures; do not use fractions (8½, 4½, etc.)
DIAGRAM
TABLE FOR CONVERTING METRES TO FEET.
Contour Interval 5 Metres
1000
2000
3000
4000
5000
6000
7000
8000
9000 Yards
9000 Metres

GLOSSARY.
TRENCH MAP.
FRANCE.
SHEET 51B S.W.
EDITION 5.A
INDEX TO ADJOINING SHEETS

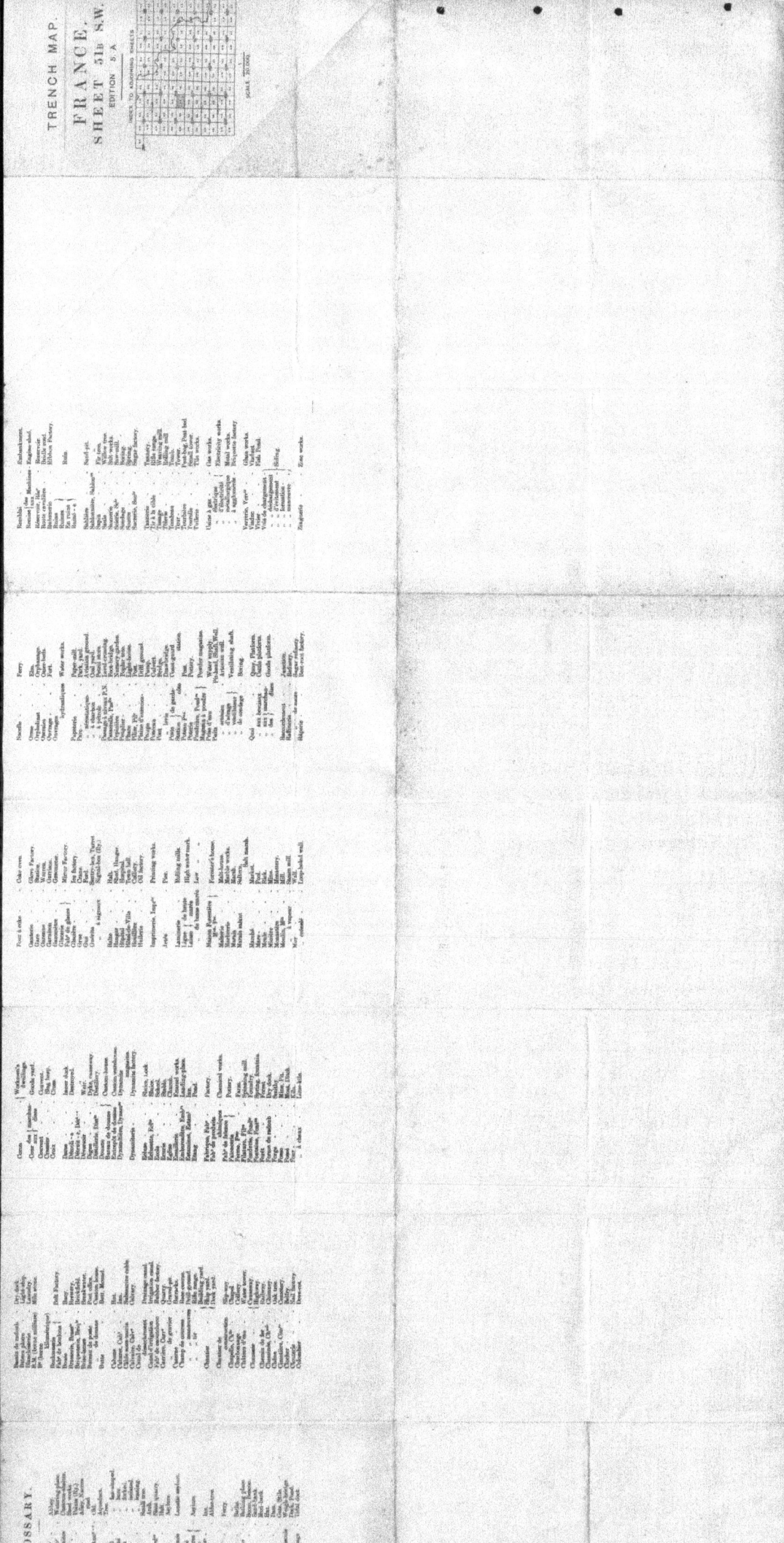

SECRET

Vol 22

# WAR DIARY.

## 102nd INFANTRY BRIGADE,

## HEADQUARTERS

## MAY 1918

Edward Williams

102 B.H.Q.
10:6:1918.

BRIGADIER-GENERAL.
COMDG: 102nd INFANTRY BRIGADE.

Instructions regarding War Diaries and Intelligence Summaries are contained in F. S. Regs., Part II. and the Staff Manual respectively. Title pages will be prepared in manuscript.

# WAR DIARY
*or*
# ~~INTELLIGENCE SUMMARY.~~

Headquarters 102nd Infantry Brigade
(Erase heading not required.)

Volume 30
May 1918

Army Form C. 2118.

| Place | Date | Hour | Summary of Events and Information | Remarks and references to Appendices |
|---|---|---|---|---|
| L12 C 0.2 | 2ND | — | O.O. 205 ISSUED. | APP I (a) |
| SHEET 27 | | | Reliefs carried out in accordance with O.O. 205. | |
| " | 4TH | – | O.O. 206 ISSUED. | APP I (b) |
| | 5TH | | Relief carried out in accordance with O.O. 206 except that 22ND Bn NORTHD. FUS on relief came under the orders of G.O.C. 101ST INF. BDE. + took over a portion of the POPERINGE system between G 20 b. 9 2 + G 4 b 9 0. | |
| K12 d 7.8. | " | | Relief completed by 7 pm + Bde H.Q. moved K 12 d 7.8 at 7 pm. 23RD NF in camp at K 12 b 6 4. 25TH NF at L 7 b 5 5. also 102ND L.T.M.B. | |
| | 6TH | | 22ND NF rejoined at 8 pm. + went into camp at L 7 d 4.2. 102ND INF BDE. became in Divisional Reserve. | |
| | | | PROVISIONAL Defence scheme issued | APP: II |
| | 12TH | | O.O. 207 ISSUED. | APP: I (c) |
| | | | 102ND INF Bde group marched in accordance with O.O. 207. Dispositions at completion of march:— | |
| | | | BDE HQ + LTMB — B 18 a 3 2 } SHEET 27 | |
| | | | 22ND NF — B 22 b 5 8 | |
| | | | 23RD NF — H 3 d 5 + 7 | |

2353 Wt. W2544/1454 700,000 5/15 D. D. & L. A.D.S.S./Forms/C. 2118.

Instructions regarding War Diaries and Intelligence Summaries are contained in F. S. Regs., Part II. and the Staff Manual respectively. Title pages will be prepared in manuscript.

# WAR DIARY
*or*
~~INTELLIGENCE SUMMARY.~~
*(Erase heading not required.)*

Army Form C. 2118.

| Place | Date | Hour | Summary of Events and Information | Remarks and references to Appendices |
|---|---|---|---|---|
| B. 8 a 3 2 | 12TH | | 18TH NF B 25 a 9 5<br>No 3 Coy 34TH DN TRAIN & 44 Mob Vet Sec B 14 c 9 4 } SHEET<br>102 FIELD AMBULANCE B 27 b 9 9 } 27 | |
| | 13TH | | O.O. 208. ISSUED at 1 AM. | APP I (a) |
| | | | Dismounted personnel moved by bus in accordance with O. O. 208. except that the debussing point was at HARLETTES (SHEET 5A HASEBROOK) Units marched from HARLETTES to billets. Transport & mounted units marched to ST. MARTIN AU LAERT & billeted there. | |
| | 14TH | | TRANSPORT resumed march & joined units. | |
| | 15TH | | CAPT M CARR M.C. assumed duties of BDE MAJOR 102ND INF BDE (from G.S.O.3. 39TH DIVISION) vice MAJOR TROBRIDGE D.S.O. (to G.S.O.2. 33RD DIVN) | |
| | | | Ordinary Training carried out by units. Selection of officers & N.C.O.s to form Battalion training Cadres. | |
| | 16TH | | Training as usual. 34th Divisional order re move of surplus personnel to BASE issued. | |
| | | | O. O. 209 issued. | APP I (b) |

Instructions regarding War Diaries and Intelligence Summaries are contained in F. S. Regs., Part II. and the Staff Manual respectively. Title pages will be prepared in manuscript.

# WAR DIARY
*or*
# INTELLIGENCE SUMMARY.
*(Erase heading not required.)*

Army Form C. 2118.

| Place | Date | Hour | Summary of Events and Information | Remarks and references to Appendices |
|---|---|---|---|---|
| | 17th | | Surplus personnel entrained at DESVRES train leaving at 10.10 a. for ETAPLES. | |
| | | | O.O. 210 issued | APP I (8) |
| | | | Officers + NCOs of training Cadre proceeded for Courses of instruction at MUSKETRY SCHOOL + XV Corps School QUESQUES. Construction platoon assembled at [illegible]. | |
| | 18th | | BDE HQ + Battalions moved in accordance with 34th Div O.O. to villages to be occupied by 55th AMERICAN BDE. Bde. HQ closed at VELINGHEM + reopened at BLÉQUIN. | |
| | 19th | | Advanced parties 55th AMERICAN BDE. arrived to take over billets in the new area. | |
| | 20th | | Training instructions issued to Bttns. | |
| | 21st | | 1st Battn 109 Inf Regt 55th Inf Bde (AMERICAN) arrived in billets at BLÉQUIN | |
| | 22nd | | More AMERICAN Troops arriving in the area | |

2353 Wt. W2544/1454 700,000 5/15 D. D. & L. A.D.S.S./Forms/C. 2118.

Instructions regarding War Diaries and Intelligence Summaries are contained in F. S. Regs., Part II, and the Staff Manual respectively. Title pages will be prepared in manuscript.

# WAR DIARY
*or*
# INTELLIGENCE SUMMARY.
*(Erase heading not required.)*

Army Form C. 2118.

| Place | Date | Hour | Summary of Events and Information | Remarks and references to Appendices |
|---|---|---|---|---|
| | 23rd | | 55th AMERICAN INF BDE arrived at BLEQUIN. Training grounds in BDE area reconnoitred. | |
| | 24th | | Preparations for training pushed forward rapidly. Two AMERICAN troops arrived in the area. | |
| | 25th | | No definite training commenced but preparations rabidly being made. O.O. 211 issued | APP 1(g) |
| | 26th | | As above. O.O. 212 issued. | APP 1(h) |
| | 27th | | No parades as the AMERICAN paraded for divine service. Orders issued by Div for training to commence on 28th. | |
| | 28th | | Training commenced including the training of the AMERICAN troops with the BRITISH SLE MK 3 rifles. BDE. HQ moved to RIPPEMONT to become more central in the training area. New BDE HQ opened at RIPPEMONT 11 am. | |

2353 Wt. W2544/1454 700,000 5/15 D. D. & L. A.D.S.S./Forms/C. 2118.

Instructions regarding War Diaries and Intelligence Summaries are contained in F. S. Regs., Part II. and the Staff Manual respectively. Title pages will be prepared in manuscript.

# WAR DIARY
*or*
# INTELLIGENCE SUMMARY.
*(Erase heading not required.)*

Army Form C. 2118.

| Place | Date | Hour | Summary of Events and Information | | Remarks and references to Appendices |
|---|---|---|---|---|---|
| | 29th | | The dispositions of 102nd Inf Bde & 55th American Inf Bde are now as follows :— | | |
| | | | 102nd Inf Bde HQ. | RAPEMONT. | |
| | | | 20th Bn North'd Fus. | BÉCOURT | |
| | | | 23rd Bn North'd Fus. | HENNEVEUX (Att'd. 103 Inf Bde) | |
| | | | 25th Bn North'd Fus. | LA CALIQUE. | |
| | | | 55th American Bde HQ. | BLÉQUIN. | Sheet. Calais. No 7. |
| | | | 109th Inf Regt HQ. | BÉCOURT. | |
| | | | 1st Bn 109th Inf Regt. | BÉCOURT. | |
| | | | 2nd Bn 109th Inf Regt. | ZOTEUX. | |
| | | | 3rd Bn 109th Inf Regt | TROIS MARQUETS. | |
| | | | 110th Inf Regt HQ. | LA CALIQUE. | |
| | | | 1st Bn 110 Inf Regt. | BLEQUIN. | |
| | | | 2nd Bn 110 Inf Regt. | SEMLECQUES | |
| | | | 3rd Bn 110 Inf Regt. | LOTTINGHEM. | |
| | | | Training still continues under supervision of British officers & NCOs | | |

Army Form C. 2118.

Instructions regarding War Diaries and Intelligence Summaries are contained in F. S. Regs., Part II. and the Staff Manual respectively. Title pages will be prepared in manuscript.

# WAR DIARY
*or*
# INTELLIGENCE SUMMARY.
*(Erase heading not required.)*

| Place | Date | Hour | Summary of Events and Information | Remarks and references to Appendices |
|---|---|---|---|---|
| | 30th | | No training carried out owing to AMERICAN troops being given a holiday on account of DECORATION DAY. | |
| | 31st | | Training resumed today. | |
| | | | Brigade Orders — Appendix I | |
| | | | Provisional Defence Scheme — Appendix II | |
| | | | CASUALTIES DURING MAY 1918 — Appendix III | |
| | | | HONOURS & AWARDS MAY 1918. Appendix IV | |

Edward Williams
BRIG. GENERAL
COMMANDING 102ND INF. BDE

10–6–18.

2353 Wt. W2544/1454 700,000 5/15 D. D. & L. A.D.S.S./Forms/C. 2118.

Appendix No. III

CASUALTIES - May 1918.

N I L.

Appendix No........IV

# 102nd INFANTRY BRIGADE.

## LIST OF HONOURS & REWARDS

## for May, 1918.

### 22nd. Bn. Northumberland Fusrs.

| OFFICERS. | AWARD. |
|---|---|
| Captn. A.W.D. Mark, D.S.O.,M.C. | 2nd. Bar to M.C. |
| 2/Lt. D.G.S. Gorrill | M.C. |

OTHER RANKS.

| | | | |
|---|---|---|---|
| 47209. | Sgt. | A.Monk, M.M. | Bar to M.M. |
| 38204. | L/Cpl. | S.Moyle | M.M. |
| 241552. | Sgt. | H.Himmel | M.M. |
| 2415. | Pte. | H.Pearson | M.M. |
| 14404. | Pte. | W.W.Archibald | M.M. |
| 919. | Pte. | A.Blyth | M.M. |
| 20/157. | Pte. | J.Bagnall | M.M. |

### 23rd. Bn. Northumberland Fusrs.

OFFICERS.

| | |
|---|---|
| Lieut. A. Pigg, M.C | BAR to M.C. |
| 2/Lt. J.P.Hughes | M.C. |
| Lieut. N.B. Pigg, M.C | Bar to M.C . |
| Captn. A.Morlidge | D.S.O. |

OTHER RANKS.

| | | | |
|---|---|---|---|
| 40778. | L/Cpl. | W.C.Rowland | M.M. |
| 2364. | Pte. | H.Porter | M.M. |
| 38121. | Sgt. | J.G. Luckie | M.M. |
| 4081. | Pte. | J.W.Harrison | D.C.M. |

### 25th Bn. Northumberland Fusrs.

OFFICERS.

| | | |
|---|---|---|
| A/Major, T.Capt. | T.McLachlan., M.C. | D.S.O. |
| A/Capt. T/2Lt. | E.J.Vipond | M.C. |
| 2nd Lieut. | G.Coleby | M.C. |
| T.2nd Lieut. | J.S.Bowmer | M.C. |

OTHER RANKS.

| | | | | | | | |
|---|---|---|---|---|---|---|---|
| 20/3162 | Pte. J.Thomson. | M.M. | | 6590. | Pte. H.Collins. | M.M. |
| * 1099 | CSM. J.Mitchell. | D.C.M. | | 38916 | Pte. H.Quarton. | M.M. |
| 47048. | Sgt. W.A.P.Rogers. | M.M. | | 6850. | Pte. E.Luke, | M.M. |
| 47066 | L/Cpl R.Munday. | M.M. | | 46998. | Pte. F.Wren. | M.M. |
| 26/1445 | Pte. J.W.White. | M.M. | | 47033. | Pte. A.J.Perry. | M.M. |
| 28433 | Pte. H.Roebuck. | M.M. | | 46064. | Cpl. F.Bailey. | M.M. |
| 235131 | Pte. J.Gass. | M.M. | | 1077. | Pte. A.Lawson. | M.M. |

*=*=*=*=*=*=*=*=*=*=*=*=*=*=*=*

SECRET

Copy No .. 13

App: 1(a)

Ref. Map Sheet 28 N.W. 1:20,000

## 102nd INFANTRY BRIGADE ORDER No. 205.

1.. 22nd N.F. will take over the whole of the 102nd Infantry Brigade front in the BRANDHOEK Line (i.e. from the DRIEGOENBEEK exclusive to the POPERINGHE - YPRES road exclusive) tonight before dark relieving the 23rd N.F. in the portion of that line between the DRIEGOENBEEK and the road in G.12.d.

2.. The Stokes Mortar in position about G.18.d.2.8. now attached to 23rd N.F. will come under the orders of O.C. 22nd N.F. on completion of the relief.

3.. All reserve S.A.A., grenades, wiring material and other trench stores now in the Right Battalion area of the BRANDHOEK Line will be handed over by 23rd N.F. to 22nd N.F. on relief. All tools in possession of 23rd N.F. will be taken by them to their new area.

4.. All other details of relief will be arranged direct between C.O's concerned.

5.. 23rd N.F. on relief will move to the area G.14.b. and G.9.c. and may occupy such billets in that area as are available. Two defended localities have been constructed in this area the trenches of which may be utilised for accomodation should there be insufficient billets.

6.. H.Q. 22nd N.F. will remain in its present position. H.Q. 23rd N.F. may remain in their present position for tonight if desired pending the selection by C.O. 23rd N.F. of a suitable H.Q. about G.8.d. There are three huts at G.8.d.9.2. which might be utilised as H.Q. for 23rd N.F. as a temporary measure.

7.. On relief 23rd N.F. will be in Brigade Reserve.

8.. Work in the BRANDHOEK Line will be continued tomorrow by 22nd N.F. in consultation with O.C. 208th Field Coy. R.E.
23rd and 25th N.F. will work on the POPERINGHE system: detailed instructions will be notified later.

9.. Completion of relief will be reported to Brigade Headquarters.

10.. O.C. 22nd N.F. will forward a sketch of his dispositions to Brigade Headquarters by 9 a.m. May 3rd.

ACKNOWLEDGE

[signature]
Major.
BRIGADE MAJOR.
102nd INFANTRY BRIGADE.

2-5-1918

Issued at 5pm to -

| | | |
|---|---|---|
| G.O.C. ........ | Copy No. | 1 |
| Brigade Major .... | " | 2 |
| Staff Captain .... | " | 3 |
| Signals .......... | " | 4 |
| Bde. T.O. ........ | " | 5 |
| 22nd N.F. ........ | " | 6 |
| 23rd N.F. ........ | " | 7 |
| 25th N.F. ........ | " | 8 |
| 102 L.T.M.B. ...... | " | 9 |
| 34th Division .... | " | 10 |
| 101 Inf. Bde ..... | " | 11 |
| 208 Fld. Co. R.E. . | " | 12 |
| Diary & File ... | " | 13 & 14 |

**S E C R E T** Copy No ... 16

App I (6)

## 102nd INFANTRY BRIGADE ORDER NO. 206

Ref. Map
Sheets
27 NE &
28 NW
1:20,000

1.. The 102nd Infantry Brigade will be relieved in the Left Subsector of the BRANDHOEK and POPERINGHE Lines by the 103rd Infantry Brigade on May 5th in accordance with the attached Table 'A'.
No. 2 Coy. 34th Bn. M.G.C. will remain in their present position and come under the orders of G.C. 103rd Infantry Brigade on his taking command of the Left Subsector on completion of the relief.

2.. On relief 102nd Infantry Brigade will march to camps in L.7. vacated by 103rd Infantry Brigade and will be in Divisional Reserve.

3.. Stokes mortars 103 L.T.M.B. to relieve those of 102 L.T.M.B. now in the ~~line~~ BRANDHOEK line will march in with 10th Lincolns; those to relieve that attached 25th N.F. and those in reserve will march in with 9th N.F.

4.. Units 102nd Infantry Brigade will provide guides at the rate of 1 per platoon to be at the road junction L.17.b.2.1. at the times stated in Table 'A'

5.. All moves will be by parties not greater than platoons at 200 yards distance.

6.. Units 102nd Infantry Brigade will hand over on relief all defence schemes, reserve S.A.A. grenades and other trench stores and will take over from Units 103rd Infantry Brigade copies of the Reserve Brigade Defence Scheme and all camp stores. Tools belonging to the mobile reserve of units will be taken out with units; all others will be handed over.
Lists of stores taken over and handed over will be forwarded to Brigade Headquarters by noon May 6th.

7.. Units 102nd Infantry Brigade will hand over to relieving Units 103rd Infantry Brigade full particulars of work in hand and proposed.

8.. The Staff Captain 102nd Infantry Brigade will arrange for parties from the personnel at Units Transport Lines to take over camps and stores and to report at the H.Q. of Units 103rd Infantry Brigade at 1 p.m. May 5th for this purpose.

9.. All other details of relief will be arranged direct between C.O's concerned.

10.. Completion of relief will be reported by wire to Brigade Headquarters.

11.. Brigade Headquarters will close at L.12.c.0.2. on completion of the relief and reopen at K.12.d.7.6. at the same hour.

ACKNOWLEDGE

[signature] Major.
BRIGADE MAJOR.
102nd INFANTRY BRIGADE.

4-5-1918
Issued at 2 p.m. to -

| | | |
|---|---|---|
| G.O.C. .......... | Copy No | 1 |
| Bde. Major ...... | " | 2 |
| Staff Captain ... | " | 3 |
| Signals ......... | " | 4 |
| Bde. T.O. ....... | " | 5 |
| 22nd N.F. ....... | " | 6 |
| 23rd N.F. ....... | " | 7 |
| 25th N.F. ....... | " | 8 |
| 102 L.T.M.B. .. | Copy No. | 9 |
| No. 2 Coy. 34th Bn. M.G.C. .... | " | 10 |
| 208th Fld Co R.E. | " | 11 |
| 34th Division ... | " | 12 |
| 101 Inf. Bde .... | " | 13 |
| 103 Inf. Bde. ... | " | 14 |
| No. 2 Coy. Div. Train | " | 15 |

Table 'A' ... To accompany 102nd Inf. Bde. Order No. 206

| Serial No. | U N I T | Relieved by | In | Time for guides. | Destination | Taking over camp from | REMARKS |
|---|---|---|---|---|---|---|---|
| 1 | 22nd N.F. with 3 Stokes mortars attached | 10th Lincolns with 8 Stokes mortars attached. | BRANDHOEK Line | 3 p.m. | Camp L.7.d.6.1. | 10th Lincolns | |
| 2 | 25th N.F. with 1 Stokes mortar attached & 4 in reserve. | 9th N.F. with 5 Stokes mortars attached | POPERINGHE Line. | 3.45 pm | Camp L.7.b.1.9. | 9th N.F. | |
| 3 | 23rd N.F. | 1st E. Lancs. | Brigade Reserve. | 4.30 pm | Camp K.12.b.8.4. | 1st E. Lancs. | |

**Note** - 102 L.T.M.B. will concentrate at camp at L.7.b.1.9.

APP I (c)

SECRET.

Copy No... 17

## 102nd INFANTRY BRIGADE ORDER No ... 207

Ref. Map
Sheet 27
1:40,000.

12 : 5 : 1918.

1. The 102nd Brigade Group will march to-day to the RUBROUCK Area (H.8.) in accordance with the attached Table A.

2. The following distances will be maintained on the march :-

Between Companies of Infantry .. 100x
Between Battalions of Infantry .. 500x
Between each Group of 6 vehicles. 25x

3. After passing the starting point each unit will halt automatically at 10 minutes to each clock hour and will resume the march automatically at each clock hour.
In addition there will be a halt of about 1½ hours about midday.

4. O.C. 22nd N.F. will detail a mounted officer and 2 N.C.O's to act as rearguard to the column and collect and march slowly all stragglers.
2 M.M.P. will report to O.C. Rearguard on passing Brigade Headquarters.
O.C. 102nd Field Ambulance will detail 1 horse ambulance to report to O.C. rearguard on passing the Cross Roads, K.12.c.6.3.

5. O.C. 102 Brigade Signals will send the correct time to each unit at least 1 hour before they are due to pass the starting point.

6. Arrival in billets and position of Headquarters will be reported by each unit of the Group to Brigade Headquarters.

7. Administrative instructions are being issued separately.

8. Brigade Headquarters will close at K.12.d.7.8. at 7.30 a.m.
Reports during the march to the head of the column.

ACKNOWLEDGE.

Major.
BRIGADE MAJOR.
102nd INFANTRY BRIGADE.

Issued at to :-

| | | | |
|---|---|---|---|
| G.O.C. | Copy No. 1 | 18th N.F. | Copy No. 10 |
| Brigade Major | " " 2 | H.Q. 34th Div. Train | " " 11 |
| Staff Captain | " " 3 | No. 3 Coy. Div. Train | " " 12 |
| Signals | " " 4 | 44th Mob. Vet. Sect. | " " 13 |
| Bde. Transport Officer | " " 5 | 102nd Field Ambulance | " " 14 |
| 22nd N.F. | " 6 | 34th Division. | " " 15 |
| 23rd N.F. | " 7 | 103rd Inf. Bde | " " 16 |
| 25th N.F. | " 8 | ---- | |
| 102nd L.T.M.B. | " 9 | | |

War Diary & File .. Copies Nos. 17 & 18

TABLE "A".

March on MAY 12th, 1918.

To accompany 102nd Inf.
Brigade Order No., 207.

| Serial No. | Troops in order of march | Starting Point Place | Starting Point Time to pass | DESTINATION | REMARKS. |
|---|---|---|---|---|---|
| 1. | Brigade Head-Quarters. 102 L.T.M.B. | Cross Roads K.12.c.6.3. | 8. a.m | RUBROUCK Area. | |
| 2. | 23rd N.F. | - ditto - | 8.5 am. | ditto | |
| 3. | 25th N.F. | Cross Roads L.1.c.9.1. | 8.5 am. | ditto | |
| 4. | 22nd N.F. | ditto | 8.20 am. | ditto | |
| 5. | 18th N.F. (less 1 Co.) | Cross Roads K.12.c.6.3. | 9 a.m. | ditto. | |
| 6. | H.Q. 34th Div. Train, No. 3 Coy. 34th Div. Train, and 44th Mob. Vet. Sect. | Road Junction K.5.b.0.8. | 9.35 am. | ditto | Joins column at WATOU CHURCH. |
| 7. | 102nd Field Ambulance. | Cross Roads K.12.c.6.3. | 9.25 am | ditto | |

NOTES :(a) 44th Mob. Vet. Section will be attached to H.Q. 34th Div. Train for the purposes of the march.

(b) Route for all units - WATOU - HERZEELE - WORMHOUDT. All units except H.Q. 34th Div. Train and No. 3 Coy. and 44th Mob. Vet. Section via. Cross Roads K.17.b.5.8.; H.Q. 34th Div. Train, No. 3 Coy. and 44th Mob. Vet. Section direct from their starting point to WATOU.

S E C R E T.

Copy No.. 18

APP I (a)

102nd INFANTRY BRIGADE ORDER No .... 208

Ref. Maps
Sheet 5.A.
HAZEBROUCK
& 13 CALAIS -
1:100,000.
Sheet 27
1:40,000.

12 : 5 : 18.

1. The dismounted portion of 102nd Brigade Group will move by bus to-morrow, May 13th, to the LOTTINGHEM Area (Sheet CALAIS) in accordance with the attached Table "A".

2. Units will march independently to the Embussing point so as to arrive there at the times stated in Table "A".

3. Transport and mounted units of 102nd Brigade Group will march to-morrow, May 13th, under Command of O.C. No. 3 Coy. Div. Train to a staging area, to be selected by O.C. No. 3 Coy. Div. Train in the vicinity of QUELMES in accordance with the attached Table "B".

On May 14th, this transport and mounted units will march and rejoin their units in the LOTTINGHEM Area; all orders for this march will be issued by O.C. No. 3 Coy. Div. Train.

Train Co. and Mob. Vet. Sec. march to LOTTINGHEM

4. Arrival in billets and position of Headquarters will be reported by each unit of the Group to Brigade Headquarters.

5. Administrative instructions are being issued separately.

6. Brigade Headquarters will close at B.18.a.6.4. at 6.30 am May 13th.

A_C_K_N_O_W_L_E_D_G_E.

[signature]
Major.
BRIGADE MAJOR.
102nd INFANTRY BRIGADE.

Issued at 1am 13th to :-

| | |
|---|---|
| G.O.C. .............. | Copy No. 1 |
| Brigade Major ....... | " " 2 |
| Staff C ptain ....... | " " 3 |
| Signals ............. | " " 4 |
| Brigade Transport Officer | " " 5 |
| 22nd N.F. ........... | " " 6 |
| 23rd " ........... | " " 7 |
| 25th " ........... | " " 8 |
| 102 L.T.M.B. ......... | " " 9 |
| 18th N.F. ............ | " " 10 |
| H.Q. 34th Div. Train .. | " " 11 |
| No. 3 Coy. Div. Train.. | " " 12 |
| 44th Mob. Vet. Section. | " " 13 |
| 102nd Field Ambulance.. | " " 14 |
| 34th Division ........ | " " 15 |
| 101st Inf. Bde ....... | " " 16 |
| 103rd Inf. Bde ....... | " " 17 |

Diary and File Copies 18 & 19

TABLE "A". Move of dismounted personnel - May 13th, 1918.

To accompany 102nd Inf. Bde. Order No. 208.

| Serial No. | Embussing Point | Troops to Embus | Time to arrive at Embus.Point | Route to Embussing Point. | Debussing Point. | DESTINATION | REMARKS. |
|---|---|---|---|---|---|---|---|
| 1. | Main Road from ZEGGERS CAPPEL to L'ERKELSBRUGGE in B.15.a. | 23rd N.F. | 7.0 a.m. | L'ERKELSBRUGGE | LOTTINGHEM. | LOTTINGHEM | |
| | | 25th N.F. | 7.5 a.m. | - ditto - | - ditto - | VERVAL | |
| | | 18th N.F. (less 150 men). | 7.10 a.m. | - ditto - | - ditto - | WATTERDALL | |
| | | 22nd N.F. | 7.15 a.m. | LES [illegible] PLIERS | - ditto - | LOTTINGHEM | |
| | | Bde. H.Q. & L.T.M.B. | 7.20 a.m | - ditto - | - ditto - | VELINGHEM | |
| 2. | - ditto - | 150 men 18th N.F. | 1.0 p.m. | L'ERKELSBRUGGE | - ditto - | WATERDALL | |
| | | 102 Field Ambulance | 1.5 p.m. | - ditto - | - ditto - | VIEIL MOULIER | |

NOTE :, An Officer of the Brigade Staff will allot busses to units at the Embussing Point.

## TABLE "B".

March for transport 102nd Brigade Group - May 13th, 1918.

(To accompany 102 Inf. Bde. Order No .. 208.

******

| Serial No. | Units in order of march | Starting Point: Place | Starting Point: Time to pass | REMARKS. |
|---|---|---|---|---|
| 1. | 23rd N.F. | Road Junction H.8.c.5.5. | 8.0 a.m. | |
| 2. | 25th N.F. | - ditto - | 8.4 a.m. | |
| 3. | 18th N.F. | Road Junction B.26.c.0.7. | 7.37 a.m. | includes halt at 7.50 a.m. |
| 4. | 102nd Field Ambulance. | - ditto - | 7.42 a.m. | - ditto - |
| 5. | 22nd N.F. | Road Junction B.22.a.0.1. | 7.15 a.m. | |
| 6. | No. 3 Coy. Div. Train. | Road Junction B.22.a.0.1. | 7.19 a.m. | |
| 7. | 44th Mob. Vet. Sect., & transport H.Q. 34th Div. Train. | - ditto - | 7.23 a.m. | |
| 8. | Transport 102 Inf. Bde. H.Q. | - ditto - | 7.26 a.m. | |

ROUTE :- RUBROUCK - LEDERZEELE - ST. MOMELIN - ST. MARTIN AU LAERT -

22nd N.F., No. 3 Coy. Div. Train - 44th Mob. Vet. Section and transport of H.Q. 34th Div. Train, Transport 102 Inf. Bde. H.Q. march to RUBROUCK via KOORNHUYS and Road Junction B.22.a.0.1.

---

SECRET.

Copy No.. 12

APP 1(c)

Ref. Map
Sheet 13
CALAIS
1:100,000.

# 102nd INFANTRY BRIGADE ORDER No. 209

16 : 5 : 1918.

1. The surplus personnel of the 102nd Infantry Brigade to be returned to the Base will entrain to-morrow, 17th instant, at DESVRES - marching there in accordance with the following :-

Starting Point - LOTTINGHEM - DESVRES Road - Road Junction immediately North of N.in ROSEQUEBRUNE.

| Time of head of Battalion passing Starting Point | | | |
|---|---|---|---|
| : | 22nd N.F. | .. | 7.30 a.m. |
| : | 23rd " | .. | 7.34 a.m. |
| : | 25th " | .. | 7.38 a.m. |

An interval of 200^x will be maintained between Battalions.

2. On arrival at DESVRES the head of the column will halt at the South-West end of the short road running in a line between the L of LES PIERREETES and first S of DESVRES.

3. An Officer from each battalion will meet the Staff Captain at the R.T.O's office, DESVRES, at 9.0 a.m. bringing with him the exact Entraining Strength. This officer will be respons-:ible for entraining his own battalion.

Time of departure of train .. 10.10 a.m.

4. Rations for consumption May 18th will be loaded in bulk on the train.

5. Transport necessary for Officers' valises and rations will march with units.

ACKNOWLEDGE.

M Carr Captain.
BRIGADE MAJOR.
102nd INFANTRY BRIGADE.

Issued through Signals - p.m.

Distribution -

| | | |
|---|---|---|
| G.O.C. ... | Copy No. | 1 |
| Brigade Major | " " | 2 |
| Staff Captain .. | " " | 3 |
| Signals ....... | " " | 4 |
| Bde. Transport Off. | " | 5 |
| 22nd N.F. ........ | " | 6 |
| 23rd " ........ | " | 7 |
| 25th " ........ | " | 8 |
| 34th Division ..... | " | 9 |
| R.T.O. DESVRES .. | " | 10 |
| No. 3 Coy. Train .. | " | 11 |
| War Diary .. | " | 12 |

SECRET.

Copy No.. 19

App I(b)

Ref. Map
Sheet 13
CALAIS
1:100,000.

102nd INFANTRY BRIGADE ORDER No .. 210

17 : 5: 18.

1. The 102nd Infantry Brigade is to be affiliated to the 55th Brigade of the 28th American Division for training purposes.

2. The 102nd Infantry Brigade comprising Brigade Headquarters, 3 Training Battalions and attached instructional staff together with transport, will move to the BLEQUIN sub-area to-morrow, the 18th instant in accordance with attached Table "A".

Billetting parties from each battalion will meet the Staff Captain at the Area Commandant's Office, BLEQUIN, at 10.0 a.m. to-morrow, 18th inst.

ø Companies as laid down in Table "B" of 34th Div. G.S. 266/13 dated 16.5.18 will proceed direct to the billets of the American Unit to which they are detailed for attachment. Instructions will be issued by the Staff Captain as to allotment of billets for and reception of American units.

3. The proposed location of units of the 55th American Brigade and billetting accommodation are shewn in Table "B" attached.

American units are expected to commence arriving about the 19th or 20th.

4. The allotment of Training Battalions will be as laid down in 34th Division G.S. 266/13 and this office letter T.S. 71/14 dated 16.5.18.

Information regarding Training Areas and facilities will be published later.

5. The Demonstration Platoon at present under the orders of O.C. 22nd N.F. will move with and be accommodated by O.C. 23rd Bn. N.F. who will be responsible for the training of the Platoon and its rationing and equipment from the 19th instant inclusive.

6. Officers and Other Ranks attending courses at the XVth Corps School, QUESQUES, will attend to-morrow the 18th inst. after which date the courses will close for this Brigade except the Caterers course. Students will be conveyed to their new billets by transport to be arranged by O.C. Battalions.

7. ACKNOWLEDGE.

M. Carr Captain.

BRIGADE MAJOR.
102nd INFANTRY BRIGADE.

Issued through Signals at 10 30 p.m.

Distribution -

| | | |
|---|---|---|
| G.O.C. .......... | Copy No. | 1 |
| Brigade Major ... | " " | 2 |
| Staff Captain ... | " " | 3 |
| 34th Division "G" | " " | 4 |
| 34th Division "Q" | " " | 5 |
| Comdt. XVth Corps School ......... | " " | 6 |
| Area Comdt. LOTTINGHEM | " | 7 |
| Area Comdt. BLEQUIN | " | 8 |
| 2/Lt. Jackson .... | " | 9 |
| 22nd N.F. ..... | Copy No. | 10 |
| 23rd " ..... | " | 11 |
| 25th " ..... | " | 12 |
| No. 3 Coy. Train | " | 13 |
| 102nd Fld. Amb.. | " | 14 |
| Signals ....... | " | 15 |
| Brigade Transport Officer ...... | " | 16 |
| 101st Inf. Bde .. | " | 17 |
| 103rd Inf. Bde .. | " | 18 |

War Diary and File .. Copies 19 & 20

ø 2 O.R's from Surplus personnel will proceed with each Coy.

P.T.O.

To accompany 102nd Inf. Bde. Order No. 210

PTO

TABLE "A"

| Serial No. | UNIT | FROM | TO | ROUTE | REMARKS. |
|---|---|---|---|---|---|
| 1 | BRIGADE HEADQUARTERS. | VELINGHEM | BLEQUIN | LOTTINGHEM STATION. | Not to pass LOTTINGHEM Station before 2.20 p.m. |
| 2 | 22nd Bn. N. F. | LOTTINGHEM | DIGNOPRE | - do - | To be clear of LOTTINGHEM Station by 2.0 p.m. |
| 3 | 23rd Bn. N.F. | LOTTINGHEM | BLEQUIN | - do - | To pass LOTTINGHEM Station at 2.10 p.m. |
| 4 | 25th Bn. N.F. | VERVALE. | LA CALIQUE | VIEL MOULIER | No to enter LOTTINGHEM before 2.30 p.m. |

Table "B" .. To accompany 102 Inf. Bde. Order No. 210

| Serial No. | AMERICAN Unit | Establishment: Off. | Establishment: O.R. | British Unit attchd. | Strength Off. | Strength O.R. | LOCATION | Accomodatn. available: Off. | Accomodatn. available: O.R. | Accomodatn. required: Off. | Accomodatn. required: O.R. | REMARKS. |
|---|---|---|---|---|---|---|---|---|---|---|---|---|
| | 55th Brigade H.Q. | 5 | 18 | 102nd Bde. H.Q. | 8 | 80 | BLEQUIN ) | | | | | |
| 1 | 1st Bn.110th Inf. Regt ........... | 26 | 1000 | 23rd N.F. 1 Coy<br>& Transport<br>Demonstration Ptn | 4<br>1<br>1 | 48<br>35<br>44 | " )<br>" )<br>" ) | 58 | 1351 | 45 | 1225 | |
| 2 | 110th Inf. Regt.H.Q.<br>Supply Coy ......... | 14<br>4 | 294<br>138 | 25th N.F.H.Q.,<br>1 Coy.& Transport | 5 | 83 | LA CALIQUE | 15 | 550 | 23 | 515 | Tents probably available. |
| 3 | 2nd Battn. 110th Infantry Regt. ..... | 26 | 1000 | 1 Coy. and Instr. Staff. | 3 | 16 | SENLECQUES. | 20 | 1000 | 29 | 1016 | - do - |
| 4 | 3rd Battn. 110th Infantry Regt. ..... | 26 | 1000 | 1 Coy. and Instr. Staff. | 3 | 16 | LOTTINGHEM. | 35 | 1500 | 29 | 1016 | -do- |
| 5 | 109th Inf. Regt.H.Q.<br>Supply Coy ........ | 14<br>4 | 294<br>138 | 22nd **N.F.** H.Q.<br>1 Coy.**&** **Transport** | 5 | 83 | DIGNOPRES | 8 | 550 | 23 | 515 | -do- |
| 6 | 1st Battn. 109th Infantry Regt. ..... | 26 | 1000 | 1 Coy. & Instr. Staff.... | 3 | 16 | BECOURT | 24 | 1133 | 29 | 1016 | -do- |
| 7 | 2nd Battn. 109th Infantry Regt. .... | 26 | 1000 | 1 Coy. & Instr. Staff ... | 3 | 16 | ZOTEUX | 37 | 1000 | 29 | 1016 | |
| 8 | 3rd Battn. 109th Infantry Regt. .... | 26 | 1000 | 1 Coy. & Instr. Staff ... | 3 | 16 | TROIS MARQUETTE<br>MIEURLIN. | 24 | 1100 | 29 | 1016 | |

APP I(9)

**SECRET.**

Ref. Sheet
CALAIS.13
1:100,000.

**102nd INFANTRY BRIGADE ORDER NO. 211** Copy No.. 14

25-8-1918

1. The Training Battalion Cadre of the 23rd Battalion Northd. Fusiliers will move to HENNEVEUX tomorrow morning, the 26th inst.
No restrictions as to time of march and route.
Rations for consumption on the 27th inst. will be carried.
No Officers or other ranks of the Brigade Instructional Staff will proceed with the Battalion.
The Demonstration Platoon will remain in its present location.

2. The 23rd Bn. Northd. Fus. will be attached to Machine Gun Companies of the 38th American Division in accordance with copy of 34th Division G.S.280/56 attached (issued to 23rd N.F. only).

3. Completion of move will be reported to this office.

23rd Bn. Northd. Fus. please acknowledge.

Captain.
BRIGADE MAJOR.
102nd INFANTRY BRIGADE.

102 B.H.Q.

Issued through Signals at 8.0 p.m.

**Distribution -**

| | |
|---|---|
| 23rd N.F. | 101st Inf. Bde. |
| Staff Captain. | 103rd Inf. Bde. |
| Bde. Transport Officer. | No. 3 Coy. Train |
| Signals. | Area Comdt. BLEQUIN. |
| 34th Division. | |
| War Diary & File. | |

SECRET

APPI(9)

Copy No .. 12

Ref Map.
Sheet 13
CALAIS, 1:100,000

102nd INFANTRY BRIGADE ORDER No. 212

26-5-18

1. The 102nd Infantry Brigade Headquarters will move from BLEQUIN to RIPPEMONT tomorrow, the 27th instant, closing at BLEQUIN at 11 a.m. and re-opening at RIPPEMONT at the same hour.
The Intelligence Bureau will remain at BLEQUIN.

2. ACKNOWLEDGE.

McCay
Captain.
BRIGADE MAJOR.
102nd INFANTRY BRIGADE.

Issued through Signals at

Distribution -

22nd N.F.
23rd N.F.
25th N.F.
101st Inf. Bde.
34th Div.
55th American Bde.
No. 3 Coy. 34th Div. Train.
103rd Infantry Bde.
102nd Field Ambulance.
Signal Officer.
Bde. Transport Officer.
--
Diary & file.

To accompany 102 Inf. Bde.
Provisional Defence Scheme.

[illegible] C.

Ref. Map
'A' attached.

1. The frontage in the [illegible] System for which 34th Division is responsible extends from the road in L.21.a. inclusive to the road at G.14.c.5.1. exclusive.

2. Should 102nd Infantry Brigade be ordered to hold this portion of the [illegible] line dispositions will be taken up as follows :-

Right Battn. .. 23rd N.F.
Centre Battn. .. 25th N.F.
Left Battn...... 22nd N.F.

Dividing lines will be :-

(a) Between Right and Centre Battalions, L.16.c.9.2. -- Road Junction L.16.a.4.6.

(b) Between Centre and Left Battalions; Road at L.17.d.9.1. - thence N.E. along road exclusive.

3. Each battalion will hold at least one Company in Battalion Reserve.

To accompany 102 Inf. Bde.
Provisional Defence Scheme.

Ref. Map
'A' attached.

SCHEME A.

1. The front of the BRANDHOEK System in the Left Subsector will be held by 25th N.F. with 4 mortars 102 L.T.M.B. attached.
H.Q. 25th N.F. will be established at G.11.d.4.1.

2. 23rd N.F. will occupy the Outpost, Front and Support lines of the POPERINGHE System in the Left Subsector and will hold the strong points at G.17.c.6.8. and G.11.a.3.3. each with 1 platoon under an Officer.
The Reserve line of the POPERINGHE System in G.9.a. is placed at the disposal of O.C. 23rd N.F. for the accommodation of his Reserve Company.
H.Q. 23rd N.F. will be at H.3.c.9.6.

3. 22nd N.F. will be disposed as follows :-

One Company in each of the defended localities in G.14.b. – G.9.c. and G.9.b.

One Company in the Reserve line of the POPERINGHE System in G.8.d. and G.14.a. and b.

H.Q. 22nd N.F. will be established at G.9.a.5.3.

H.Q. 102 L.T.M.B. and 4 mortars will be in reserve at H.Q. 22nd N.F.

4. Brigade Headquarters will be established at L.12.c.0.2. with Advanced Report Centre at G.16.d.8.9.

To accompany 102 Inf. Bde.
Provisional Defence Scheme.

---

Ref. Map
'A' attached.

SCHEME B.

1. The front of the BRANDHOEK System in the Left Subsector will be held by 23rd N.F. on the Right and 25th N.F. on the Left.

Dividing line between battalions :-

Farm at G.18.b.8.8. inclusive to Left Battalion — Road Junction G.11.c.5.1.

Each battalion will hold at least one Company in Battalion Reserve.

2. H.Q. 23rd N.F. G.17.b.2.0.
H.Q. 25th N.F. G.11.d.4.1.

3. 3 mortars 102 L.T.M.B. will be attached to 25th N.F. and one to 23rd N.F.

4. 22nd N.F. will occupy the POPERINGHE System in the Left Subsector and will hold the strong points at G.17.c.5.8. and G.11.a.5.3. each with 1 platoon under an Officer.

H.Q. 22nd N.F. will be at G.9.a.5.6.
H.Q. 102nd L.T.M.B. and 4 mortars in reserve will be with H.Q. 22nd N.F.

5. Brigade Headquarters will be established at L.12.c.0.2. with Advanced Report Centre at G.16.d.5.8.

---

SECRET. APP: II Copy No.. 13

# 102nd INFANTRY BRIGADE PROVISIONAL DEFENCE SCHEME.

Ref. Maps
Sheets 27 N.E. and
28 N.W. 1:20,000.

8th May, 1918.

1. The front in the BRANDHOEK and POPERINGHE lines which 34th Division may be called upon to hold is bounded on the South by the line H.1.b.9.2. — G.29.d.9.7. — G.25.b.3.2. — L.22.c.7.6. and on the North by the POPERINGHE—YPRES Road exclusive.

2. One Infantry Brigade (at present 103rd Infantry Brigade) is occupying the BRANDHOEK and POPERINGHE Systems as follows :-

   One Infantry Battalion holding 10 small posts in the BRANDHOEK System in the Divisional area - remainder of battalion in billets close in rear.

   Two Infantry Battalions billetted about the POPERINGHE System.

3. One Infantry Brigade (at present 102nd Infantry Brigade) is in Divisional Reserve in L.7. and K.12.

   One Infantry Brigade (at present 101st Infantry Brigade) is in Divisional Reserve in the HOUTKERQUE area.

4. In the event of 34th Division being ordered to hold the BRANDHOEK line, 102nd Inf. Bde. will take over the Left Subsector relieving the troops of 103rd Inf. Bde. in that area.

4. continued -

103rd Infantry Brigade is then to hold the Right Subsector.

101st Infantry Brigade is then to move to the area L.15.b. and d. and remain in Divisional Reserve.

5. The dividing line between the 2 Infantry Brigades in the BRANDHOEK System will be :-

G.24.b.5.2. -- Cross Roads BUSSEBOOM, G.18.c.60.15 (inclusive to Right Brigade) -- Road Junction G.14.b.9.0. thence Eastwards along Grid line.

6. In the event of 102nd Infantry Brigade being ordered to hold the Left Subsector of the BRANDHOEK Line this will be done in accordance with either of the attached Schemes A or B as will be notified at the time.

7. O.C's units will cause routes from the present Camps to the BRANDHOEK System to be reconnoitred by as many Officers as possible.

8. If the 102nd Infantry Brigade is ordered to hold the ABEELE Line this will be done in accordance with the attached Scheme C.
O.C's units will reconnoitre the portions of the ABEELE System allotted them for defence and will select positions in which to establish their Headquarters.
The position of Brigade Headquarters will be notified later.

[signature]

Inf. . 102. BRIGADE MAJOR. Major.

Distribution of :-

102nd INFANTRY BRIGADE

PROVISIONAL DEFENCE SCHEME.

---

| | | | | |
|---|---|---|---|---|
| G.O.C. | ..... | Copy | No. | 1 |
| Brigade Major | .. | " | " | 2 |
| Staff Captain | .. | " | " | 3 |
| Signals | ...... | " | " | 4 |
| Bde. Transport Officer. | | | " | 5 |
| 22nd N.F. | .... | " | " | 6 |
| 23rd " | ... | " | " | 7 |
| 20th " | ... | " | " | 8 |
| 102 L.T.M.B. | .. | " | " | 9 |

---

| | | | | | |
|---|---|---|---|---|---|
| 34th Division | ..... | " | " | 10 | for |
| 101st Inf. Bde | ... | " | " | 11 | infor- |
| 103rd Inf. Bde. | .. | " | " | 12 | mation. |

---

Diary and File .. Copies Nos. 13 and 14.

---

(6339) Wt. W160/M3016. 1,500,000 10/17 McA & W Ltd (E 1898) Forms W3091.

Army Form W.3091.

# Cover for Documents.

---

**Nature of Enclosures.**

---

**Notes, or Letters written.**

WM 30

# WAR DIARY & APPENDICES

JUNE - 1918

H. QRS. 102nd INF. BRIGADE

Instructions regarding War Diaries and Intelligence Summaries are contained in F. S. Regs., Part II. and the Staff Manual respectively. Title Pages will be prepared in manuscript.

# WAR DIARY
*or*
~~INTELLIGENCE SUMMARY~~
*(Erase heading not required.)*

VOL. XXXI

Army Form C. 2118.

JUNE 1918

102nd Inf. Brigade

| Place | Date | Hour | Summary of Events and Information | Remarks and references to Appendices |
|---|---|---|---|---|
| Ref. MAP SHEE 13 CALAIS 1/100,000 | 1.6.18 | | Training of AMERICANS units continued. | |
| | 2.6.18 | | O.O. 213 issued. The 102nd Inf Bde HQ & 23rd Bn NF moved by march route to the HARDINGHEN area & were affiliated to 155th Inf Bde 78 AMERICAN DIVN. for training purposes. Dispositions as under:–<br>102nd Inf. Bde. HQ. HARDINGHEM<br>23rd Bn NORTH'D FUS. BOURSIN.<br>No 3 Coy TRAIN HARDINGHEM. | App No 1 (a) |
| | 3.6.18 | | The following training cadres arrived & came under the command of GOC 102nd Inf Bde.<br>13th Bn EAST SURREY REGT. HARDINGHEN<br>12th Bn YORKS REGT. BOURSIN<br>21st Bn MIDDLESEX REGT. WACQUINGHEN | |
| | 4.6.18 | | Advanced parties of the AMERICAN UNIT arrive in the area. | |
| | 5.6.18 | | AMERICAN units arrived in the area. | |

2449 Wt. W14957/M90 750,000 1/16 J.B.C. & A. Forms/C.2118/12.

Instructions regarding War Diaries and Intelligence Summaries are contained in F. S. Regs., Part II. and the Staff Manual respectively. Title Pages will be prepared in manuscript.

# WAR DIARY
*or*
# INTELLIGENCE SUMMARY
*(Erase heading not required.)*

Army Form C. 2118.

102nd Inf. Brigade

| Place | Date | Hour | Summary of Events and Information | Remarks and references to Appendices |
|---|---|---|---|---|
| Ref Map 13 CALAIS 1:100000. | 6.6.18 | | Training commences of AMERICAN UNITS. | |
| | 7.6.18 | | Training continues as usual. | |
| | 8.6.18 | | | |
| | 9.6.18 | | | |
| | 10.6.18 | | O.O 214 issued to 102nd INF Bde. The own units moved by march route to the [illegible]NGTHUN area & were disposed as follows to train Machine Gun & Engineer units of the AMERICAN DIVN (78th) | APP No 1(6) |
| | | | BRITISH UNITS. — AMERICAN UNITS. — LOCATION | |
| | | | 102nd INF Bde HQ — — ALINCTHUN CHATEAU. | |
| | | | 22nd BN N.F — 308th M G BN — BOURSIN | |
| | | | 23rd BN NF — 304th DIVN M G BN, 309 & 310 REGL M G COYS — BOURSIN | |
| | | | 25th BN N.F. — 309 M G BN, 311 & 312 REGL M G COYS — LE WAAST | |
| | | | 18th BN NF — 303rd ENGINEER REGT — ALINCTHUN | |

2449 Wt. W14957/M90 750,000 1/16 J.B.C. & A. Forms/C.2118/12.

Instructions regarding War Diaries and Intelligence Summaries are contained in F. S. Regs., Part II. and the Staff Manual respectively. Title pages will be prepared in manuscript.

# WAR DIARY
*or*
# INTELLIGENCE SUMMARY.
*(Erase heading not required.)*

Army Form C. 2118.

| Place | Date | Hour | Summary of Events and Information | Remarks and references to Appendices |
|---|---|---|---|---|
| Ref Map Calais 13 1/100,000. | 11.6.18 | | Training of the AMERICAN units affiliated to the 102nd were commenced Lt Col H A MEEVES D.S.O. M.C. assuming command (of 102nd Inf Bde) | |
| | 12.6.18 | | Training proceeds. | |
| | 13.6.18 | | | |
| | 14.6.18 | | | |
| | 15.6.18 | | O.O. 215 issued | App No 1(c) |
| | 16.6.18 | | O.O. 216 issued | App No. 1(d) |
| | 17.6.18 | | The 102nd Inf Bde moved by march route to ROSEMEL CHATEAU ½ mile S of FRENCQ (CALAIS 13 b.c 30.62) in accordance with operation order 216. All Bn Training Cadres of 102nd Inf Bde passed to the command of 18th Bde. Lt Col H A MEEVES D.S.O. M.C. remained in command of the Bde during the absence of the G.O.C. The 102nd Inf Bde took over training cadres of the 16th Divn training units of the 7o" AMERICAN Divn. Dispositions as follows – | |
| | | | BRITISH UNITS — LOCATION | |
| | | | 102nd Inf Bde HQ — ROSEMEL CHATEAU | |

2353 Wt. W2544/1454 700,000 5/15 D. D. & L. A.D.S.S./Forms/C. 2118.

Instructions regarding War Diaries and Intelligence Summaries are contained in F. S. Regs., Part II. and the Staff Manual respectively. Title pages will be prepared in manuscript.

# WAR DIARY
*or*
# ~~INTELLIGENCE SUMMARY.~~
*(Erase heading not required.)*

Army Form C. 2118.

| Place | Date | Hour | Summary of Events and Information | Remarks and references to Appendices |
|---|---|---|---|---|
| Ref MAP Sheet 13 Calais 1:100,000 | 17.6.18 | | BRITISH UNITS — LOCATION<br>4TH (S.I.H.) BN ROYAL IRISH REGT — FRENCQ<br>4TH BN LINCOLNSHIRE REGT — HALINGHEM<br>AMERICAN UNITS — LOCATION<br>313TH M.G. BN — LE TURNE<br>314TH M.G. BN — FRENCQ<br>315TH M.G. BN — FRENCQ<br>317TH M.G. COY — HUBERSENT<br>318TH M.G. COY — HUBERSENT<br>319TH M.G. COY — HUBERSENT<br>320 M.G. COY — HUBERSENT | |
| | 18.6.18 to 26.6.18 | | Training of the American units was [illegible] and [illegible] the [illegible]. | |
| Ref Map 13 Calais 15a Hazebrouck 1:100000 | 27.6.18 | | O.O. 217 issued.<br>1st Bn Lincolnshire Regt took over the duties of 102ND INF Bde Training Cadres 4th Lincolns & 8th RIR<br>[illegible] 4 (S.I.H.) Bn Royal Irish came under command of [illegible] Inf Bde | APP No 1 (?) |

2353 Wt. W2544/1454 700,000 5/15 D. D. & L. A.D.S.S./Forms/C. 2118.

Instructions regarding War Diaries and Intelligence Summaries are contained in F. S. Regs., Part II. and the Staff Manual respectively. Title pages will be prepared in manuscript.

# WAR DIARY
*or*
~~INTELLIGENCE SUMMARY.~~
*(Erase heading not required.)*

Army Form C. 2118.

| Place | Date | Hour | Summary of Events and Information | Remarks and references to Appendices |
|---|---|---|---|---|
| Ref Map Sheet 13 Calais. 5a Hazebrouck 1. 100,000. Sheet 19 1: 40,000. | 28.6.18 | | 102nd Inf Bde moved in accordance with O.O. 27 by lorry to Pont de Wylder V 25 a 5.7 sheet 19 1:40,000. Transport moving by road to the St Momelin area (Hazebrouck 5a). | |
| | 29.6.18 | | O.O. 28 issued. | App. No 1 (8) |
| Ref Map Sheets 19 + 27 1 40,000. | 30.6.18 | | 102nd Inf Bde HQ moved by march route in accordance with O.O. 28 to Oost Cappel sheet 19. 1:40,000. Transport continued its march from St Momelin area to Bambecque area. Dispositions of the Bde were as follows.<br>102nd Inf Bde HQ — Ost Cappel<br>14th Bn Cheshire Regt — Hofland. E 2 b 80. 30. (Sheet 27)<br>1/7th Bn Cheshire Regt. — Bambecque V. 28 b 10. 30. (Sheet 19)<br>1/1st Bn Hereford Regt. — Les 5 Chemins. (Sheet 19)<br>205th Field Coy RE. — V 18 d 20. 10. (Sheet 19) | |

2353 Wt. W2544/1454 700,000 5/15 D. D. & L. A.D.S.S./Forms/C. 2118.

Army Form C. 2118.

Instructions regarding War Diaries and Intelligence Summaries are contained in F. S. Regs., Part II. and the Staff Manual respectively. Title pages will be prepared in manuscript.

# WAR DIARY
*or*
# INTELLIGENCE SUMMARY.
*(Erase heading not required.)*

| Place | Date | Hour | Summary of Events and Information | Remarks and references to Appendices |
|---|---|---|---|---|
| | | | Operation Orders attached —— Appendix 1 | |
| | | | Disposition Reports —— Appendix 2 | |
| | | | Casualties during June 1918 —— Nil | |
| | | | Honours and Awards – June 1918 —— Appendix 3 | |
| | | | [illegible signature] | |
| | | | Brigadier General, Commanding 102nd Inf Bde | |

Appendix No. 3

# HONOURS & AWARDS - JUNE, 1918.

## 22nd Bn. North'd. Fus.

D. C. M.

46105 L/Cpl. A.Ellis.
30824 L/Cpl. S.Royle.

M. M.

266003 Pte. T.Jefferson.
64844 Pte. R.Bell.
36783 Pte. C.Tolson.
22/1057 Sgt. T.Poulton.

## 23rd Bn. North'd. Fus.

"SECOND BAR" TO M.C.

Lieut. N.B.Pigg.

MILITARY CROSS.

2/Lieut. F.H.Viner.
Lieut. D.E.Ward.

D.C.M.
23/822 Sgt. G.A.Cowans.
40304 Sgt. W.Whitehead.

BAR TO "M. M."
20/190 Pte. J.T.Johnson.

M. M.
23/44 L/Cpl. W.R.McLachlan.
21/938 Pte. J.Maston.
59379 Pte. C.F.Barker.
23/976 L/Cpl. T.Carr.
37334 Cpl. A.Clayton.
21/817 L/Cpl. A.Jackson.

## 25th Bn. North'd. Fus.

MILITARY CROSS.
2/Lieut. G.Coleby.

D. C. M.
46027 Pte. A.Jacques.

M. M.
60780 Sgt. C.Laycock.
8318 Cpl. T.Nichol.
30/131 Cpl. W.Duck.
38878 Cpl. F.Goldthorpe.
38821 L/Cpl. R.Pickles.
46766 L/Cpl. W.Telfer.
47312 Pte. H.Gent.
235139 Pte. T.Laycock.

*=*=*=*=*=*=*=*=*=*=*=*=*=*=*=*=*=*=*=*=*=*=*=*

SECRET.

APPENDIX No 1 (a)
Copy No.. 20

Ref. Map
Sheet 13,
CALAIS
1:100,000.

# 102nd INFANTRY BRIGADE ORDER No.. 213

2 : 6 : 1918.

1. The 102nd Infantry Brigade Headquarters together with the Battalion Training Cadre of the 23rd Bn. North'd. Fusiliers and No. 3 Coy. Div. Train, are to be affiliated to the 155th Infantry Brigade of the 78th American Division for training purposes.

2. The training cadres of the 22nd and 25th Bns. North'd. Fusiliers together with all attached instructors, and the H.A.C. and 102nd Bde. Demonstration Platoons will remain in present locations and come under the orders of the 101st Infantry Brigade at 10.0 a.m. on June 3rd.

The H.A.C. and 102nd Bde. Demonstration Platoons will be attached to the 22nd Bn. North'd. Fusiliers.

The 2 Officers and 10 N.C.O. Signalling Instructors at present with Signal School at BLEQUIN will move with Brigade Headquarters to the new area.

3. (a) 102nd Infantry Brigade Headquarters and the instructors from the Signal School will be formed up on the RIPPEMONT-SENLECQUES Road facing W. with the head of the column at Brigade Headquarters at 7.0 a.m. on June 3rd. and will proceed by march route to HARDINGHEN -

Route - SENLECQUES - LOTTINGHEN - VELINGHEN - SELLES -
BRUNEMBERT - LONGUEVILLE - HADRIEGHEN -
COLEMBERT - BOURSIN.

2/Lt. Wilkins, attached H.Q. 102nd Inf. Bde. will be in charge of the column.

Packs will be carried on the transport and will be at Bde. Transport lines by 6.0 a.m. to-morrow, 3rd inst.

The kits of Officers proceeding by march route will be at Bde. Headquarters ready for loading by 7.0 a.m. 3rd inst.

(b) The 23rd Bn. North'd. Fusiliers will move from HENNEVEUX to BOURSIN on the morning of the 3rd inst. under orders to be issued by O.C. 23rd Bn. N.F.

(c) No. 3 Coy. Div. Train will move from SENLECQUES to HARDINGHEN on June 3rd under orders of O.C. Train.

(d) Rations for consumption on June 4th will be carried.

(e) Arrivals at destinations will be reported to Brigade Headquarters.

4. On the arrival in the HARDINGHEN Area 3 new training Cadres will be attached to the 102nd Inf. Bde. and these together with the 23rd Bn. N.F. will be affiliated to American Units as given in 34th Div. G.S. 270/4 of 31.5.18 forwarded under this office T.S. 78/1 dated 1.6.18. Proposed locations of American units and orders as to allotment of instructors will be issued later

5. Brigade Headquarters will close at RIPPEMONT at 10.0 a.m. and reopen at HARDINGHEN at an hour to be notified later.

6. Acknowledge.

M Carr Captain.
BRIGADE MAJOR.
102nd INFANTRY BRIGADE.

Distribution -

Distribution -

102nd Inf. Bde. Order No.. 213

| | | |
|---|---|---|
| G.O.C. ......... | Copy No. | 1 |
| Brigade Major .. | " " | 2 |
| Staff Captain .. | " " | 3 |
| Bde. Transport Off. | " " | 4 |
| O.C. 102 Bde. Signals | " | 5 |
| 2/Lt. Wilkins .... | " " | 6 |
| 22nd N.F. ......... | " " | 7 |
| 23rd " ......... | " " | 8 |
| 25th " ......... | " " | 9 |
| O.C. No. 3 Coy. Train | " | 10 |
| O.C. 102 Bde. Demonstration Platoon | " | 11 |
| O.C. H.A.C. - do - | " | 12 |
| H.Q. 101st Inf. Bde | " | 13 |
| H.Q. 103rd Inf. Bde | " | 14 |
| H.Q. 34th Division | " | 15 |
| Area Comdt. BLEQUIN | " | 16 |
| 102nd Field Amb. .. | " | 17 |
| 104th Field Amb. .. | " | 18 |
| H.Q. 55th American Bde. | " | 19 |
| War Diary & File .. | Copies | 20 & 21 |

SECRET.

APPENDIX No1(b)

Copy No 22

Ref. Map CALAIS 13 1:100,000

102nd INFANTRY BRIGADE ORDER No.. 214

10:3:18.

1.. As soon as the 28th American Division has left its present area the 78th American Division will be concentrated in the LUMBRES Area, part of BLEQUIN Area and at BOURSIN.

2.. The 102nd Infantry Brigade composed as under will be affiliated to the Machine Gun and Engineer Units of the 78th American Division for training purposes as follows :-

| BRITISH UNIT. | AMERICAN UNIT. | LOCATION. |
|---|---|---|
| 102nd Inf. Brigade Headquarters ..... | | ALINCTHUN CHATEAU. |
| 22nd Bn. N.F. .... | 306th M. G. Battn...... | BOURSIN. |
| 23rd Bn. N.F. .... | 307th Divn. M.G. Battn. 309th & 310th Regtl. M. G. Coys .......... | BOURSIN. |
| 25th Bn. N.F. .... | 309th M. G. Battn ..... 311th & 312th Regtl. M. G. Coys .......... | LE WAST. |
| 18th Bn. N.F. .... | 303rd Engineer Regt ... | ALINCTHUN. |

3.. The move of units at present under the orders of 102nd Infantry Brigade will be carried out in accordance with Table "A" attached. 23rd Bn. N.F., 307th Divn. M.G. Battn. and 309th Regtl. M.G. Coy. will remain in present locations. Instructors of the 23rd Bn. N.F. at present with the 22nd and 25th Bns. N.F. will rejoin their Unit on arrival in the new area.

Units who are to come under the orders of the 102nd Inf. Brigade will move under the orders of G.O's. C. Brigades under whom they are now serving.

The 102nd Brigade Demonstration Platoon will proceed to ALINCTHUN and will be attached to Brigade Headquarters.

Signal instructors will remain attached to Brigade Headquarters.

4.. Brigade Headquarters will close at HARDINGHEN at 10.0 a.m. on 12th inst. and reopen at ALINCTHUN CHATEAU at the same hour.

ACKNOWLEDGE.

M Carr
Captain.
BRIGADE MAJOR.
102nd INFANTRY BRIGADE.

Issued through Signals at 8 p.m.

Distribution -

| | | | |
|---|---|---|---|
| G.O.C. ........... | Copy | No. | 1 |
| 22nd N.F. ......... | " | " | 2 |
| 23rd " ......... | " | " | 3 |
| 25th " ......... | " | " | 4 |
| 13th Yorks Regt ... | " | " | 5 |
| 13th E. Surrey Regt. | " | " | 6 |
| 21st Middlesex Regt. | " | " | 7 |
| Staff Captain ..... | " | " | 8 |
| Signal Officer .... | " | " | 9 |
| Bde. Transport Off.. | " | " | 10 |
| -- | | | |
| 34th Division ...... | " | " | 11 |
| 101st Inf. Bde ..... | " | " | 12 |
| 103rd Inf. Bde ..... | " | " | 13 |
| -- | | | |
| 78th American Division. | " | " | 14 |
| 307th Divn. M.G. Bn... | " | " | 15 |
| 309th Regtl. M.G. Coy. | " | " | 16 |
| 3rd Bn. 309th Inf. Regt. | " | " | 17 |
| -- | | | |
| Area Commandant, BOURSIN | " | " | 18 |
| " " HARDINGHEN. | " | " | 19 |
| " " ACQUINGHEN | " | " | 20 |
| -- | | | |
| No. 3 Coy. Train ....... | " | " | 21 |
| -- | | | |
| War Diary & File.. | Copies | | 22 & 23 |

TABLE "A". To accompany 102 Bde. Order No. 214.

| Ser. No. | Date | UNIT | FROM | TO | ROUTE | |
|---|---|---|---|---|---|---|
| 1 | 11.6.18 | 13th Bn. EAST SURREY Regt. | HARDINGHEN. | BAYENGHEN. | Any | |
| 2 | 11.6.18 | 13th Bn. YORKS Regt...... | BOURSIN. | BLEQUIN. | Any | Billets to be taken over by 22nd N.F. |
| 3 | 11.6.18 | No. 3 Coy. Train | HARDINGHEN. | HENNEVEUX. | Any | |
| 4 | 11.6.18 | 21st Bn. MIDDLESEX Regt.. | WACQUINGHEN. | HAUT LOQUIN. | Any | Staging night 11/12th at HARDINGHEN. |
| 5 | 12.6.18 | 102nd Inf. Bde. Headquarters .. | HARDINGHEN. | ALINCTHUN CHATEAU. | LE VERT MONT LE WAST ALINCTHUN. | |

AMERICAN UNITS.

| Ser. No. | Date | UNIT | FROM | TO | ROUTE | |
|---|---|---|---|---|---|---|
| 6 | 11.6.18 | Supply Coy. 309th Inf. Regt. | WACQUINGHEN | ALQUINES. | Any | Staging night of 11/12th at HARDINGHEN. |
| 7 | 11.6.18 | 3rd Battn. 309th Inf. Regt. | BEUVREQUEN | HAUT LOQUIN | Any | - ditto - |

APPENDIX No 1 (d)

SECRET. Copy No.. 18

Reference
CALAIS Map
1/100,000.

# 102nd INFANTRY BRIGADE ORDER No.. 216.

16th June, 1918.

1.. The 34th Divisional Cadre (less all Battalion Cadres) will move to the SAMER Area on the 17th instant and take over the training of the 80th American Division from the 16th British Division.

2.. The 102nd Infantry Brigade Headquarters with strength as per War Establishment plus 1 Intelligence Officer with batman, will move from ALINCTHUN CHATEAU to ROSAMEL CHATEAU ½ mile S. of FRENCQ (CALAIS 80 3062) closing at the former place at 9.0 a.m. and re-open at an hour to be notified later.

Lieutenant-Colonel H.H. NEEVES, D.S.O., M.C., will remain in Command of the 102nd Infantry Brigade during the absence of the G.O.C.

3.. The Battalion Training Cadres of the 102nd Infantry Brigade will come under the orders of the 116th Inf. Brigade in accordance with copies of 39/G/27/1 attached (forwarded to 18th, 23rd and 25th Bns. North'd. Fusiliers).

4.. Orders as to the disposal of surplus personnel of Brigade Headquarters, 22nd N.F. and of the Demonstration Platoon will be issued later.

5.. Orders for move of 22nd N.F. will be issued when date of embarkation has been received.

6.. Acknowledge.

[signature] Captain.
BRIGADE MAJOR.
102nd INFANTRY BRIGADE.

Issued at 4.0 p.m.

| Copy No. | | | |
|---|---|---|---|
| 1 | O.C. 102 Bde. | 8 | 18th N.F. |
| 2 | Bde. Major. | 9 | 22nd N.F. |
| 3 | Staff Captain. | 10 | 23rd N.F. |
| 4 | O.C. 102 Bde.Signals. | 11 | 25th N.F. |
| 5 | Bde. Transport Off. | 12 | 34th Div. |
| 6 | Bde. Intell. Off. | 13 | 101st Inf. Bde. |
| 7 | O.C. 102 Bde. Demonstration Platoon. | 14 | 103rd Inf. Bde. |
| | | 15 | Area Comdt. HENNEVEUX. |
| | | 16 | No. 3 Coy. Train. |
| | | 17 | Bde. Supply Officer. |

War Diary and File .. Copies 18 & 19.

APPENDIX No 1 (e)

SECRET.

Copy No..

Ref. Maps
Sheet 13
CALAIS - 1:100,000.

Sheet 5A. -
HAZEBROUCK - 1:100,000.

**102nd INFANTRY BRIGADE ORDER No.. 217**

27 : 6 : 1918.

1.. The 34th Division is being transferred to the II Corps Second Army.
117th Infantry Brigade (H.Q. SAMER) is taking over the duties of the 34th Division in connection with the 80th Division A.E.F.

2.. The 102nd Infantry Brigade will move by lorry from ROSAMEL CHATEAU to PONT DE WYLDER, V.25.a.5.7. (Sheet 19) on the 28th instant.

3.. The 4th Battn. Lincoln Regiment will come under the orders of the G.O.C. 117th Infantry Brigade (H.Q. SAMER) at 7.0 p.m. 27th instant.
Captain HOLMES, M.C. Commanding 4th Bn. Lincoln Regiment will take over the duties of 102nd Infantry Brigade in connection with Engineer and Machine Gun Units of 80th American Division.
4 Company Cadres from 8th K. R. R. C. will take over on the 27th instant the affiliation recently carried out by 7th (S.I.H.) Bn. Royal Irish Regiment with American Machine Gun Units and will come under the orders of O.C. 4th Bn. Lincoln Regiment.

4.. 102nd Infantry Brigade Headquarters will close at ROSAMEL CHATEAU at 9.0 a.m. 28th instant and re-open at PONT DE WYLDER at an hour to be notified later.

5.. Acknowledge.

M. Carr Captain.
BRIGADE MAJOR.
102nd INFANTRY BRIGADE.

Issued through Signals at 7.0 p.m.

Distribution -

Copy No. 1 G.O.C.
2 Brigade Major
3 Staff Captain.
4 Intelligence Officer.
5 O.C. Demonstration Platoon.
6 No. 3 Coy. Train.
7 Bde. Supply Officer.
8 Area Comdt. FRENCQ.
9 8th Bn. K. R. R. C.
10 4th Lincolns.
11 117th Inf. Bde.
12 34th Division.
13 D.O.R.E. - FRENCQ.

American Units -
14 313th M. G. Battn.
15 314th "
16 315th "
17 317th Regtl. M.G. Coy.
18 318th "
19 319th "
20 320th "

War Diary & File .. 21 & 22 .

APPENDIX No 1(8)

SECRET.

Copy No.. 1

# 102nd INFANTRY BRIGADE ORDER No. 218

29th JUNE 1918.

Ref. Map
HAZEBROUCK.
1:100,000.

1.. The 102nd Infantry Brigade Group, composed of units shown in attached March Table, will march from ST. MOMELIN Area to BAMBECQUE Area on the 30th inst.

2.. March will be carried out in accordance with Table attached.

Distances will be observed on the march as follows :-

100 yards between each ~~vehicle~~ UNIT.
25 yards between every six vehicles.

3.. Billeting parties from each unit will meet the Staff Captain at the Area Commandant's Office, BAMBECQUE, at 10.0 a.m. on the 30th inst.

4.. 102nd Infantry Brigade Headquarters will move from PONT DE WYLDER to OOST CAPPEL on the 30th inst., closing at 11.30 a.m. and reopening at the latter place at the same hour.

5.. Units will report arrival in the new area giving location of H.Q. to Brigade Headquarters.

6.. Major RUSSELL, M.C. Comdg. 208th Field Coy. R.E. will be in charge of the column.

7.. Acknowledge.

[signature]
Captain.
BRIGADE MAJOR
102nd INFANTRY BRIGADE.

Copies to -

1 War Diary
2 File
3 Transport Off. 1/1st Hereford Regt.
4 Transport Off. 1/4th Cheshires.
5 Transport Off. 1/7th Cheshires.
6 No. 3 Coy. Train.
7 O.C. Bde. H.Q. Mounted Portion.
8 102nd Fld. Amb.
9 208th Fld. Co. R.E.
10 34th Div.
11 Area Comdt. BAMBECQUE.

MARCH TABLE -- To accompany 102 Inf. Bde. Order No.218

STARTING POINT -- Cross Roads half mile S. of last E in LEDERZEELE.

Date ... 30.6.18.

| Serial No. | UNIT | FROM | TO | Head of Column to pass S. P. | ROUTE. | REMARKS. |
|---|---|---|---|---|---|---|
| 1 | T'port Detls 1/1 Hereford Regt......... | ST. MOMELIN Area. | OOST CAPPEL | 8 a.m. | E in BROXEELE - ZEGGERS CAPPEL - ESQUELBECQ - HERZEELE - BAMBECQUE. | |
| 2 | T'port Detls. 1/4 Cheshires | -do- | HOFLANDE | 8.5 am | | |
| 3 | T'port Detls 1/7 Cheshires | -do- | BAMBECQUE WEST | 8.10 am | | |
| 4 | No. 3 Coy. Div. Train... | -do- | Farms near ROUSBRUGGE Camp. | 8.15 am | | |
| 5 | Mted.Portion Bde. H.Q.... | -do- | OOST CAPPEL. | 8.20 am | | |
| 6 | 102nd Fld. Amb. | -do- | KRUYSTRAETE | 8.25 am | | |
| 7 | 208 FldCo.R.E. | -do- | Farms near 2000x N.W. of BAMBECQUE. | 8.35 am | | |

App.No 2

SECRET. No.. 1

Ref. Maps
Sheets 19 & 27
1:40,000.

DISPOSITION REPORT
30.6.18

Scherpenberg Camp 2.3.e.98

102nd INFANTRY BRIGADE HEADQUARTERS .. OOST CAPPEL
(Billet No. 50)

1/4th Bn. Cheshire Regt ............. HOFLAND, E.2.b.80.30

1/7th Bn. Cheshire Regt ............. BAMBECQUE, V.28.b.10.50.

1/1st Bn. Hereford Regt. ........... LES CINQ CHEMINS.

102nd Field Ambulance ............... LA KRUYSTRAETE.

No. 3 Coy. Train ...................... W.20.b.00.50.

208th Field Coy. R.E. ................ V.18.d.20.10.

M Carr
Captain.
BRIGADE MAJOR.
102nd INFANTRY BRIGADE.

102 B.H.Q.
30:6:1918.

SECRET. Copy T.S. 21/5

Headquarters,
34th Division.

DISPOSITION REPORT.
22:6:18.

| | | |
|---|---|---|
| British Units. | BRIGADE HEADQUARTERS .... | ROSAMEL CHATEAU. |
| | 7th (S.I.H.) Bn. Royal Irish Regiment .................... | FRENCQ. |
| | 4th Bn. Lincolnshire Regt.... | HALINGHEM. |
| American Units. | 313th Machine Gun Battn...... | LE TURNE. |
| | 314th Machine Gun Battn...... | FRENCQ. |
| | 315th Machine Gun Battn...... | FRENCQ. |
| | 317th Machine Gun Coy........ | HUBERSENT. |
| | 318th Machine Gun Coy........ | HUBERSENT. |
| | 319th Machine Gun Coy........ | HUBERSENT. |
| | 320th Machine Gun Coy........ | HUBERSENT. |

M Carr Capt
for
Lieutenant-Colonel.
COMDG: 102nd INFANTRY BRIGADE.

102 B.H.Q.
22:6:1918.

www.ingramcontent.com/pod-product-compliance
Lightning Source LLC
Chambersburg PA
CBHW081541160426
43191CB00011B/1813

* 9 7 8 1 4 7 4 5 1 7 0 4 1 *